Oasis Center Library
317 East Call Street
Tallahassee, Florida 32301

The Intimate Friendships of Elizabeth Ann Bayley Seton

1 - Elizabeth Ann Seton

DEDICATION

to

MY FAMILY, MY FRIENDS

and

my religious community,

THE SISTERS OF CHARITY,

especially

MOTHER M. VICTORIA BROWN

The Intimate Friendships of Elizabeth Ann Bayley Seton

First Native-Born American Saint (1774-1821)

Sr. Marie Celeste, SC

ALBA · HOUSE NEW · YORK
SOCIETY OF ST. PAUL, 2187 VICTORY BLVD., STATEN ISLAND, NEW YORK 10314

Library of Congress Cataloging-in-Publication Data

Marie Celeste, Sister, S.C.
    The intimate friendships of Elizabeth Ann Bayley Seton, first native-born American saint (1774-1821) / Sister Marie Celeste.
       p.   cm.
    Bibliography: p.
    Includes index.
    ISBN 0-8189-0555-7
    1. Seton, Elizabeth Ann, Saint, 1774-1821 — Friends and associates. 2. Christian saints — United States — Biography.
    I. Title.
BX4700.S4M37   1989
271'.9102 — dc20   89-6647
[B]   CIP

Designed, printed and bound in the United States of America by the Fathers and Brothers of the Society of St. Paul, 2187 Victory Boulevard, Staten Island, New York 10314, as part of their communications apostolate.

© Copyright 1989 by the Society of St. Paul

Printing Information:

Current Printing - first digit 1 2 3 4 5 6 7 8 9 10 11 12

Year of Current Printing - first year shown
  1989   1990   1991   1992   1993   1994   1995   1996

FOREWORD

If it is true that one's friendships best reveal one's inmost life, then to know the friendships of a saint is to achieve a penetrating look into the heart of that person. But often enough one knows little about these friendships. Only rarely, as in this book, does the reader enter deeply into the heart of the saint through such friendships.

What makes this book particularly fascinating is that it reveals the intimate everyday details of growing friendships — details which at first may seem insignificant or overly homey but which later, bit-by-bit form a mosaic of warm beauty. Thus Sister Marie Celeste lets Elizabeth Ann Seton tell us, frequently in her own words, how she dealt with her friends in day-to-day laughs and tears and in times of domestic peace and academic crisis. In so doing, the author painstakingly sketches the intimate moments of Elizabeth Ann Seton's often stormy, never dull, life.

Because Elizabeth is allowed to speak for herself not only in direct quotations but also in condensed versions of her many long letters, the language is often the more precious style of the late seventeen nineties and early eighteen hundreds. Yet this does not veil her sometimes biting humor to a local prelate or her playful manner with Eliza Sadler or her tender affection for Antonio Filicchi or her constant craving for a Cecilia Seton's companionship or her simple delight in her husband's ardent affection.

We are fortunate, then, that Sister Marie Celeste had not only the courage to ransack the various archives for over five years to discover these intimate details of Elizabeth Ann Seton's life but also the honesty to reveal in them her strengths and weaknesses. This gives us all hope as we struggle to find Christ in all the details, often messy, of our own daily living.

DAVID J. HASSEL, S.J.
Loyola University of Chicago
March 25, 1987

CONTENTS

Foreword by David J. Hassel, S.J. v

Introduction ix

  Chapter 1: The Life-Long Context of
Elizabeth Ann Seton's Friendships
— A Biographical Sketch 3

  Chapter 2: Nature Reveals
God's Friendship for Me 21

  Chapter 3: My Father: My First Friend 33

  Chapter 4: William Magee Seton:
My Husband and Friend 45

  Chapter 5: Antonio Filicchi:
My Friend becomes My Brother 71

  Chapter 6: Rebecca Seton: My
Sister-in-Law and Dearest Friend ... 91

  Chapter 7: Julia Scott: My Worldly Half
and Friend in Every Need 101

  Chapter 8: Cecilia Seton: My Spiritual Half
and Inseparable Friend 117

  Chapter 9: Catherine Dupleix and Eliza Sadler: My
Never Failing New York Friends ... 129

  Chapter 10: Simon Gabriel Bruté: My Priest-Friend
and My Final Strength 141

Epilogue by David J. Hassel, S.J. 159

Appendix: The Parents of Students become more than mere Acquaintances for Elizabeth Ann Seton 165

Abbreviations 181

End Notes 183

Bibliography 193

Index 201

INTRODUCTION

From many diverse viewpoints, people have written about Elizabeth Ann Seton, a prolific writer and our first native-born American saint. *The Intimate Friendships of Elizabeth Ann Seton*, a companion book to *Elizabeth Ann Seton: A Self-Portrait; A Study of Her Spirituality in Her Own Words*, views her from her extraordinary capacity for friendship as expressed in her letters and personal diaries.

When a child, Elizabeth discovered that God was her most intimate friend, always present in the events of the times, the happenings of her daily life, and the people she encountered. Because she was intensely present to others as well as to God, her friendships became more numerous than the ten described here.

Her life naturally divides into two major phases, those before and after her conversion to the Catholic faith.

The first phase includes her early friendship with God in nature, with her father (Dr. Richard Bayley), with her husband (William Magee Seton), with her New York and Philadelphia friends, Catherine Dupleix, Eliza Sadler and Julia Scott, and with her sisters-in-law, Rebecca and Cecilia Seton.

The second phase shows how her growing friendship with God led her to embrace those whose support made it possible for her to be received into the Catholic community, later to found Saint Joseph's Academy for Girls and still later, to establish her religious community of Sisters of Charity. These friends include both Antonio Filicchi of Leghorn, Italy, and the Reverend Simon G. Bruté, her confessor and the spiritual director of her religious community in Emmitsburg, Maryland.

While her friendships among the parents of her students, namely the O'Conways, the Harpers and the Foxes and her Baltimore friends may not be called intimate, yet they were more than mere acquaintanceships. At times, Elizabeth Seton had confided to them her personal cares and concerns. In return, they, too, had reciprocated this trust. Hence the account of their friendships is given in the Appendix.

An introductory sketch will provide the background for the friendships of her life. Her complete life-story may be found in *Elizabeth Ann Seton: A Self-Portrait* (cf. Selected Bibliography).

I wish to express again my gratitude to those friends whose encouragement and assistance made the publication of my studies on Elizabeth Ann Bayley Seton possible: Pope Paul VI for his blessing on these two works and to his private secretary, Monsignor Pasquale Macchi, at whose request they were written; to the Reverend William W. Sheldon, C.M., Postulator-General for the Cause of Saint Elizabeth Ann Seton; to the late John Cardinal Wright for a travel grant obtained from the Medora A. Feehan Fund.

A special word of acknowledgment is due the Reverend David J. Hassel, S.J., author, lecturer and research professor at Loyola University of Chicago, for his continued interest in this work, for his insights and helpful suggestions, and for writing the Foreword and Epilogue to this book; to Doctor

INTRODUCTION   xi

Thomas Bennett, Director of Research Services at Loyola University of Chicago for his support in obtaining the Arthur J. Schmitt grant and for providing typing services; to Doctor Alice B. Hayes, Vice-President for Academic Affairs at Loyola University of Chicago for an honorarium; to Sister Rita Stalzer, C.S.J., and the Loyola University Library Staff for library assistance; to Joyce Dinello, Director of Art and Photography, Media Services of Loyola University; to Sisters M. Aloysia and John Mary, archivists at Saint Joseph's Provincial House, Emmitsburg, Maryland; and to the archivists of the Sisters of Charity Mother Houses for access to original letters and memorabilia, at Seton Hill, Greensburg, Pennsylvania, at Mount Saint Joseph's, Cincinnati, Ohio, at Saint Elizabeth's Convent Station, New Jersey, at Mount Saint Vincent's, New York and at Halifax, Nova Scotia.

Further, I am grateful to Monsignor Hugh J. Phillips, archivist at Mount Saint Mary's College, Emmitsburg, Maryland, and to the archivists of Mount Saint Mary's Special Collections; to the archivists at Saint Mary's Seminary and at the Archdiocesan Chancery, Baltimore, Maryland; to the archivists at Notre Dame University, Indiana, and at the Bruté Memorial Library, Vincennes, Indiana; to the late Rev. John Sullivan, S.S., curator of Elizabeth Seton's house on Paca Street, Baltimore, Maryland; to the Daughters of Charity at Saint Joseph's for their warm hospitality; to the Sisters of Charity of Seton Hill for their unfailing support; to my family and friends, notably, to Irene Prestipino, to the late Edwin Cudecki, to Dr. and Mrs. John M. O'Malley, to Anthony Recchia and Michael Spencer; to the Reverends Monsignori Thomas E. Madden and Joseph M. O'Toole, to the Reverends Eamon Carroll, O. Carm., Walter Krolikowski, S.J., Frederick L. Moriarty, S.J. and Anselm

Romb, O.F.M. Conv., for their encouragement and interest in Saint Elizabeth Ann Seton. A special word of thanks to Mrs. Natalie F. Hector for typing the manuscript.

SISTER MARIE CELESTE, S.C.
Seton Hill, Pennsylvania
Loyola University of Chicago

The Intimate Friendships of Elizabeth Ann Bayley Seton

CHAPTER 1

The Life-Long Context Of Elizabeth Ann Seton's Friendships:
A Biographical Sketch

Elizabeth Ann Bayley Seton, a child of the American Revolution, was born in New York City on August 28, 1774. She was the second of three daughters born to Dr. Richard Le Conte Bayley and Catherine Bayeux Charlton (daughter of the Episcopalian minister of Saint Andrew's Church in Richmondtown, Staten Island). Elizabeth was scarcely three years old when her mother died. This event drew her closer to her father and a strong bond of friendship began to form between them.

After Dr. Bayley's second marriage, this time to Charlotte Amelia Barclay, Elizabeth's early years were spent chiefly with her father's brother, William Le Conte Bayley, on his farm in New Rochelle, New York, a French Huguenot settlement. Here she formed many of her first friendships in the companionship of her Bayley cousins and her French relatives, the Le Contes and the Besleys. Here, too, she learned to love nature.

As she grew and matured to womanhood, she enjoyed reading the Bible and her favorite pastoral poetry. During the several occasions when her much-loved father had gone to London, England, to further his study of medicine, Elizabeth gradually learned to commune with God who thus became her most intimate friend.

By the time Elizabeth was sixteen years old, her father had achieved fame as a doctor and a surgeon. On his return to New York after one of his prolonged stays in London, Dr. Bayley opened a Health Establishment on Staten Island to care for the poor Irish immigrants held in quarantine. Later, he was named the first Health Officer of New York City and subsequently occupied the first Chair of Anatomy at King's College, now Columbia University.

At seventeen, while attending a society ball at the New York home of the wealthy De Lanceys, Elizabeth Bayley, then "the belle of New York," met William Magee Seton, a descendant of the Parbroath branch of Scotland's royal family and the son of a wealthy international merchant, William Seton, Sr. Elizabeth's and William's interest in each other drew immediate attention. Thereafter, they met frequently in the homes of mutual friends, the Sadlers and the Atkinsons. After a reasonably long courtship, Elizabeth, not yet twenty, and William, soon to be twenty-six, were married in New York on January 25, 1794, in the home of her sister, Mary Post. Within ten years, they became the parents of five children: Anna Maria, William, Richard, Catherine Josephine and Rebecca.

In 1798, only four years after their happy marriage, Elizabeth Seton and her husband began to suffer a series of family reverses. At the death of William Seton, Sr., Elizabeth's husband became the family representative and director of his father's business affairs, the Seton-Maitland shipping firm. The Seton household, particularly the care of William's three youngest sisters, Rebecca, Harriet and Cecilia, was confided to Elizabeth, her father-in-law's family favorite.

Not long after Mr. Seton's death, William and Elizabeth received the shocking news of the Maitland foreclosures in London and Hamburg. Reverberations were felt also in New York. William, in delicate health, began to fail noticeably. Upon the advice of creditors, after three years of harassing settlements, Seton-Maitland and Company filed bankruptcy.

Meanwhile, in caring for the poor victims of yellow fever, Elizabeth's father, Dr. Bayley, also fell victim to the illness. Thus, in a short time, Elizabeth Seton suffered not only the loss of her father and first friend, but also the impoverishment of the Seton business reverses and of her husband's failing health.

When the Setons' financial situation seemed somewhat improved, Elizabeth's main concern became the recovery of her husband's health. Looking for a warmer climate for William's incipient tuberculosis, Elizabeth and William decided to go to Leghorn, Italy. They would take with them their eldest daughter, Anna Maria; but the boys, William and Richard, and Catherine Josephine, their second daughter, were placed in the care of Elizabeth's sister-in-law, Rebecca Seton and her friend, Eliza Sadler. The one-year-old Rebecca was cared for at the home of Elizabeth's sister, Mary Post. In Leghorn, the Setons would be the guests of the Filicchi brothers, Filippo and Antonio, long-time business partners and friends of the Setons. They were to become Elizabeth's first Catholic friends.

On October 2, 1803, leaving New York Harbor for Leghorn, Italy, the Setons set sail on the *Shepherdess*. While crossing the Atlantic Ocean, Elizabeth, attentive to William's needs, felt God's protecting care of them. She wrote her friends, Julia Scott, Eliza Sadler and Rebecca Seton that William's health seemed to be improving.

Unfortunately, when they arrived at the port of Leghorn about the middle of November, the Setons were not permitted to disembark because of the yellow fever epidemic in New York City. Instead, the health authorities required that they be transferred to a prison-like Lazaretto off the Leghorn harbor, and be held in quarantine for one month. The Filicchis, disappointed at such action, did all in their power to provide as many comforts as possible to make the Lazaretto apartment liveable for them. They, likewise, provided the attention of their own physician and the services of a man-servant to take care of the meals.

In the Lazaretto, William's condition worsened, but Elizabeth was able to use the occasion to lead William to God and even to help him feel that it might be "sweet" to die. A week before Christmas, the Setons waited anxiously to be discharged. The day of their release from the Lazaretto, the Filicchis came with their carriage to remove them to an elegant apartment in Pisa, fifteen miles away. Here, rather than show signs of improvement, William passed through a week of painful tossings and agonized sufferings. As Elizabeth knelt at his bedside in prayer, William died without a groan two days after Christmas. With loving care, she prepared his body for burial. On the same day, accompanied by Mrs. Filicchi, she rode back to Leghorn where William's remains were translated for burial in the English Protestant cemetery.

While arrangements were being made for Elizabeth's and Anna's return to New York, they lived with the family of Antonio Filicchi, the deceased William's closest friend. Friendship gradually formed between Elizabeth and the thoughtful, generous Antonio who made sure she knew how to make the sign of the cross over herself and her troubles. From Amabilia, Antonio's wife, Elizabeth learned much about the practices of the Catholic faith. Recognizing her growing interest in the faith, the Filicchis challenged her to pray and inquire more deeply into the Catholic religion.

Meanwhile, in order to acquaint Elizabeth and Annina (Anna Maria Italianized) with their culture, the Filicchi wives, Amabilia and Mary (Cowper) planned for them a tour of Florence and the neighboring towns. Among the sites they would visit were the many art-filled churches. Impressed by the intense devotion of the people, Elizabeth became more and more enamored of the Catholic faith. The propitious moment of faith came for Elizabeth during a visit to the Shrine of Our Lady of Grace in Montenero, a short distance from Leghorn. At the consecration of the Mass in Our Lady's special chapel, Elizabeth bent to the floor and expressed for the first time her belief in the real presence of Jesus in the Eucharist.

In February 1804, while on board the *Shepherdess* waiting for the ship's return to New York and thinking only of seeing her children, Elizabeth again met with disappointment. Annina was found with scarlet fever. Advised to leave the ship, the Setons were again welcomed into the home of Antonio Filicchi. Later, Elizabeth also contracted the illness. She wrote Rebecca that if she could know the care and attention they had received from everybody, "it would melt her heart." The Filicchis deemed the delay providential; it offered the opportunity for Elizabeth to learn more about the Catholic faith and to strengthen her bond of friendship with the Filicchis.

Passage for the Seton's return home was finally booked on the *Pyomingo*, to leave Leghorn on April 8, 1804. As the departure date neared, the Filicchis became concerned about Elizabeth's and Annina's safety in travelling back to New York unaccompanied. To resolve the matter, they agreed among themselves that Antonio should accompany the Setons back to New York and at the same time look into their business ventures in the New World.

On the morning of their departure, Elizabeth went to Mass at the Church of Santa Catarina with Antonio and Amabilia. Then, while standing on the balcony of the Filicchi home, she embraced Amabilia and the children, Georgino and Patrizio, whom she dearly loved, bidding them goodbye. Down at the harbor, Filippo Filicchi and Guy Carleton, Elizabeth's half-brother, were waiting for them with letters for America. There, Filippo imparted his blessing and threw out to her his last challenge: "I meet you on the day of Judgment."[1]

While the voyage across the Atlantic, which lasted fifty-six days, was uneventful, it was not without problems. For Elizabeth and Antonio became deeply attracted to each other during the long trip. But strengthened by grace and faithful to prayer, Elizabeth recognized in the temptations that had beset her the work of the "enemy of salvation," and felt that the Lord was with them.

The *Pyomingo* docked in New York Harbor on June 4, 1804. As Elizabeth was greeted at the wharf by her children and friends, she learned that Rebecca Seton, for whom she had kept her Leghorn Journal, was very ill and at the point of death. Elizabeth hastened to her bedside. A month later, when the moment of death came and God called Rebecca, Elizabeth was with her as she gave "her last sigh, without a groan."

Left without Rebecca who would have been her best support in New York, Elizabeth faced many problems alone. When her Protestant relatives and friends heard that she wanted to become a Catholic, they abandoned her to her doubts and scruples. Her one-time friend, the Rev. Mr. Hobart, the Episcopalian minister at Trinity Church in New

York, thinking her stubbornly set on her course, saw her no more.

While within herself Elizabeth vacillated and remained undecided about her faith, Antonio Filicchi left New York to carry on his business affairs in Boston and Montreal. Before leaving, however, he had introduced Elizabeth to Father Matthew O'Brien, at Saint Peter's Church on Barclay Street and had recommended her to the care of Fathers John Cheverus and Francis Matignon, his cherished Bostonian friends, to whom Elizabeth later wrote for direction and advice. Antonio had previously written on her behalf to Bishop John Carroll of Baltimore.

In response to Elizabeth's letter, Father Cheverus advised her to join the Catholic Church as soon as possible, since she had heard enough arguments on both sides. To settle her disturbed mind, he wrote:

> I believe you are always a good Catholic. The doubts which arise in your mind do not destroy your faith, they only disturb your mind. . . .[2]

Thus, Elizabeth made her formal act of abjuration on March 14, 1805, and was admitted to the "true Church of Jesus Christ" that day. A copy of the *Following of Christ* [also known as the *Imitation of Christ*] which she gave Antonio was inscribed with these words: "To Antonio Filicchi from his dear sister and friend, Eliza A. Seton, to commemorate the happy day he presented her to the Church of God, the 14th March, 1805."[3] In May of the next year, Bishop John Carroll of Baltimore went to New York to administer to her the sacrament of confirmation.

As an impoverished widow, Elizabeth sought means to eke out a living for herself and her children. The three attempts to engage herself in educational projects resulted in failure: first, as house-mother to a group of boys at St. Mark's curate; then, as an associate to Mr. and Mrs. Patrick White attempting to establish a school in her home; lastly, as director of care for a select group of boys enrolled in the school of Rev. Mr. Harris, an Episcopalian minister. In each case, the failure was brought about by the talk of her former friends who greatly distrusted her conversion to the Catholic faith.

To ease Elizabeth's hardships, Antonio Filicchi authorized his creditors, J. Murray and Sons of New York, to release yearly the sum of $400.00 to Elizabeth for the education of her boys, William and Richard. He further authorized her to draw on his funds whatever amount was necessary to meet her needs. Without delay, at the suggestion of the Rev. J.S. Tisserant, a New York friend, William and Richard were sent to Georgetown College under the supervision of Bishop John Carroll.

Previously, Antonio Filicchi had suggested that Elizabeth move to Canada where she might place her sons for schooling in Montreal, find shelter for herself and her daughters in a convent-school, and perhaps assist with the teaching. But neither Father Cheverus nor Filippo Filicchi agreed to this move. While these plans were being considered, Elizabeth chanced to meet the Rev. William DuBourg, president of Saint Mary's College in Baltimore, who had stopped at Saint Peter's in New York while on his way to Boston to visit his friend, Fr. Cheverus.

When Fr. DuBourg heard about Elizabeth's plans to move to Montreal, he invited her to Baltimore to carry through his plan to open a school for girls. After much praying and seeking advice from Cheverus and Matignon, and with the concurrence of Bishop Carroll, Elizabeth felt that under their direction she was doing God's will and acquiesced to Fr. DuBourg's invitation. Cheverus had written her:

> We think that the plan of Fr. DuBourg will be much more advantageous than any yet proposed to you. It will be advantageous not only to the interests of your family, but to those of our holy religion in the United States.[4]

During Elizabeth's four years of struggle and hardships in New York, she had been gratified that several of her early friends remained faithful. After the death of her sister-in-law, Rebecca, Elizabeth's spirits had been raised when she received a touching letter from Julia Scott of Philadelphia, a cherished friend of her father, Doctor Bayley. Hearing of her financial plight, the remarkable Julia Scott offered her monetary assistance.

Catherine Dupleix and Eliza Sadler (nicknamed Dué and Sad) also proved faithful friends. In the early years of the happy marriage to the then wealthy William Seton, Elizabeth had had the leisure to spend many bright days and sparkling evenings with them and her sister-in-law, Rebecca Seton. When Elizabeth had been house-mother at Saint Mark's curate and was accused of proselytizing the boys in her care by imposing on them her religious beliefs, Dué and Sad had defended her position against their well-meaning Episcopalian minister, the Rev. Mr. Hobart.

Elizabeth's sisters-in-law, Harriet and Cecilia Seton, became her last family tie in New York. Both of them had been making their home with Protestant relatives, but Cecilia, under the direction of Fr. Michael Hurley at Saint Peter's Church in New York, had managed to be baptized a Catholic and had been attending services at Saint Peter's. Harriet, too, had leanings towards Elizabeth's religion, but when the idea was frowned upon by relatives, Harriet had given it up, but only for a time.

In early June 1808, Elizabeth and her three daughters left New York on the *Grand Sachem*, a packet, which arrived at Baltimore Bay a week later, on the feast of Corpus Christi. They were met by carriage in the rain and taken to Saint Mary's Chapel. When Elizabeth heard Fr. Hurley's voice as he intoned the *Kyrie Eleison*, she felt assured that she was among friends.

The new home at Paca Street adjoining the chapel had been prepared to receive Elizabeth and her daughters. By the Fall of 1808, Elizabeth had begun her school for girls without reference to color, race or creed. Then, when the idea of founding a religious community of women to maintain the school was introduced, by June 1809, Elizabeth had accepted several young ladies as candidates for the sisterhood: Cecilia O'Conway and Mary Ann Butler of Philadelphia (friends of Father Babade), and Susan Clossy and Maria Murphy of New York. Thus, within a year after her arrival in Baltimore, Elizabeth had started both her school and religious community. Several days later, the candidates for the sisterhood donned the habit of the Sisters of Charity, a widow's dress similar to the one Elizabeth had been wearing.

On the feast of Corpus Christi, June 16, 1809, Elizabeth and the Sisters appeared publicly for the first time at Mass in the seminary chapel wearing the habit that would identify the "Mother Seton Sisters of Charity" for more than a century and a half. A few days prior to this event, Elizabeth's sisters-in-law, Cecilia and Harriet Seton, had come to Baltimore to live with her.

In the meantime, a seminarian convert, Mr. Samuel Sutherland Cooper, became interested in Elizabeth Seton's projects and wanted to further her work. For this purpose, he purchased the Fleming farm in Emmitsburg, Maryland, a distance of fifty miles from Baltimore, where the Sulpician Fathers had earlier opened Mount Saint Mary's College for Boys. To give the ailing Cecilia Seton the benefit of the mountain air, Elizabeth set out in a covered wagon for Emmitsburg on the feast of Saint Aloysius Gonzaga, June 21, 1809, with a small group including her daughter Anna, Sister Maria Murphy and her sisters-in-law, Cecilia and Harriet. Three days later, the travelers reached Emmitsburg only to find that the farmhouse in the valley was not ready for occupancy. They crossed the road and climbed to the mountaintop where they were greeted graciously by the Rev. John DuBois, founder of the college. For shelter, he offered them the Sulpician Retreat House where the group remained for five weeks, making it their first home in Emmitsburg.

Harriet frequently accompanied Elizabeth and Cecilia up the mountainside on their way to the chapel, but usually stayed outside to wander about in the woods or to sit upon a rock and wait for them. Then one evening her desire to enter the Catholic Church became inflamed. On July 22, 1809, the feast of Saint Mary Magdalene, Harriet was happily received into the Catholic community. At the end of July, on the feast of Saint Ignatius of Loyola, Elizabeth and the rest of her group moved to the farmhouse (later called the Stone House) in the valley.

From the beginning, the Stone House proved inadequate for the needs of Elizabeth's school and sisterhood. With little delay, plans were completed to build a log house (later called the White House) which would serve the needs both of the religious community and of the school. Elizabeth had named the farmland, "Saint Joseph's Valley"; the sisterhood was officially known as the "Sisters of Charity of Saint Joseph's." By May 1810, the school was formally established and given the title "Saint Joseph's Academy for Girls."

Despite the many hardships and problems Elizabeth had encountered in founding her religious community and in establishing Saint Joseph's Academy, she experienced great joy in watching the "mustard seed" grow, a seed of faith that God had planted with the hands of Antonio, her truest friend and shepherd. Within a short time, so many young ladies sought admittance that Elizabeth had to refuse some for lack of room. She wrote Antonio that she could have filled another house as large as the White House with Sisters and children.

Elizabeth had not only the care of her growing religious community, but also the care of her own children. William and Richard had moved from Saint Mary's College, Baltimore, to Mount Saint Mary's College in Emmitsburg, while Annina, Catherine Josephine and Rebecca remained with Elizabeth at the Academy. One of her greatest delights in this arrangement was the weekly family reunion on Wednesday when her sons came to spend time at Saint Joseph's Valley. She wrote Julia Scott:

> What would I give if at this very moment you could see your own friend [Elizabeth] with the five playing all sorts of fancies round her in a bright sun, and as merry as the larks, skipping over the meadows before us.[5]

At times, the Sisters joined in the fun with the happy group. The day Richard turned fourteen, he declared to Elizabeth:

> When I look at the Sisters and think of the happy days when we were little and we could run in their arms I am obliged now to turn away. I feel so sorry we are grown up and they do not treat us as children.[6]

As foundress of the Sisters of Charity, Elizabeth Seton felt a keen responsibility to carry out God's will for the infant community. Discouraged by the many conflicts incurred through her relationship with several priest-directors of the community, she wanted to leave the charge of the Sisters and devote herself exclusively to the care of her own children. She informed Bishop Carroll of her decision; if only her own happiness was in question, she would have said: "How good is the cross for me. This is my opportunity to ground myself in patience and perseverance."[7] But Elizabeth's greater concern was the painful situation the Sisters were experiencing.

At first Bishop Carroll would have conceded to Elizabeth's desires, but later he appreciated how great would be the disappointment of admiring Catholics, if anything should happen to shake her holy establishment, and he wrote her:

> I declare an opinion and belief that the ultimate success under God depends on your sacrificing yourself, notwithstanding all the uneasiness and disgust you may experience, and continuing in your place as Superior.[8]

As if expressly sent by God to support Elizabeth, the Rev. Simon Gabriel Bruté, soon to be known as the "Angel of the Mountain," was appointed assistant to Fr. DuBois, the last named superior of the Sisters. Fr. Bruté, whom Elizabeth addressed fondly as *G*, soon found a cherished place in her heart. Elizabeth opened herself freely to him, often urging him to tell her what she might do to prove better her love for God. She told him things that she would ordinarily have carried hidden within her to the grave.

In the beautiful valley of Saint Joseph, Elizabeth's thoughts frequently turned to death and eternity. She recalled the years in New York when despite the estrangement from her Protestant relatives, she had attended six of them in their last agony within the space of two years. Among them were her half-sister, Emma Bayley Craig; her step-mother, Charlotte Amelia Bayley; Eliza Maitland (William's half-sister); and Mary Hoffman Seton (wife of James Seton, William's brother). In the throes of death, they had been horrified, and had called for her comforting presence.

So, Elizabeth was somewhat ready when death became a frequent visitor in Saint Joseph's Valley. In less than a year after their arrival in Baltimore, God claimed the cherished souls of Harriet[9] and Cecilia Seton. After a brief and unsuccessful romance, Anna, too, on whom Elizabeth doted, fell victim to the family complaint, tuberculosis.[10] Elizabeth's youngest daughter, Rebecca, light-hearted, smart, sensible, was left entirely lame, as the consequence of a serious fall on the ice. Despite the best services of the famed Baltimore and Philadelphia physicians, after three years of excruciating pain, praying day and night, Rebecca died in Elizabeth's arms.[11]

During all this time, Elizabeth's life was being lost in God. The many contradictions, anxieties and sufferings endured in New York and at Saint Joseph's took a toll on her health. She wrote Julia Scott and Catherine Dupleix that she was "worn out." The pain in her chest made it difficult for her to write. Without cough or expectoration, it gave her an almost continual slow elevating fever. Only the superabundance of love and good nursing that she had received from those around her and the advice of Dr. Chatard kept her going. When Julia Scott invited Elizabeth to come to be with her in Philadelphia, she answered:

> I would not leave my little common habits, comforts and enjoyment of books, pen, etc. in my present state of health; besides, the blow it would be to the heart of my sister [Mary Post] if I should leave home and not put myself under my Brother Post's [Dr. Wright Post's] skill and care.[12]

In response to their goodness and their confidence in her, Elizabeth confided many of her anxieties to her ever-faithful Baltimore friends: Fr. Babade, Mrs. Chatard, George Weis and Matthias O'Conway. They were aware of the times her heart was heavy about many things. She told Fr. Babade that he could not appreciate her miseries, "no love of vocation, no pure charity, no assimilation with holy poverty, no pliancy of spirit." Even before the Tabernacle, all was so quiet that she wondered whether she was simply in love with her misery. She wrote Mrs. Chatard that she tried to hide her ungrateful heart even from her best friends, since she knew nothing could justify or even excuse its depression. She told George Weis how the painful whispers of her being dismissed as Mother of the community on behalf of Sister Rose White's nomination had put the Sisters in a fearful state of mind. To Matthias O'Conway, she wrote that she suffered like a child. While laughing with one eye, she wept with the other.

Though in pain and suffering herself, Elizabeth tried by peaceful cheerfulness to bring her friends comfort and consolation. She was far prouder of her alliance with Mr. O'Conway than if she had been mistress of the universe. The sign of God's love for him was his family sorrow. To lighten George Weis' sufferings, she wrote him that he must know he did not suffer alone. She wanted him to look up to the Master Carpenter he followed and not give way to dejection. "Calvary is the rendez-vous . . . for true souls; there my dear George both you and I must meet Him." She had also asked him to tell Fr. Babade that she was afraid to do the least to ease her pains for fear they might be sent to him. She knew one or the other must be nailed fast to the cross.

In September 1820, while workers were constructing an addition to the White House for a day school, Elizabeth suffered a severe setback. She had climbed a pile of boards to see the progress the workmen had made when a sharp wind struck her. Not being well, she contracted a strong fever from the exertion. Several days later, Fr. DuBois anointed her. She wrote Sister Betsey in New York to tell her about it and added: "The getting well is slow." Blowing and puffing, Elizabeth had taken nearly a day to write the letter.

Elizabeth's health now had noticeably declined, but until the very end, she had tried to keep her interests alive. Confined to her room, she wanted to know the progress of each child in the school. Their loud laughing and playing brought her new life. A visit from her son Richard, then in the Navy, also brought her much happiness. With Sister Cecilia O'Conway, she talked about many things: the pain of separation, death, departed friends, present suffering compared to suffering in purgatory. "I am ashamed to complain," she said, "when I remember those dear ones who have gone. What agonies they must have suffered!"[13]

On New Year's Day, 1821, Fr. Bruté visited her briefly after Benediction, found her very low and gave her absolution. The next day, when Fr. Bruté and the Sisters feared that Elizabeth might die during the night, Fr. DuBois arrived in the afternoon to administer Extreme Unction. Catherine Josephine and the Sisters gathered around her bedside to join in the prayers. Lifting her faint voice to thank them for their kindness in being present at that trial, she asked their forgiveness for the scandals she may have given them. Then, with a heaving breast, she repeated: "Be children of the Church. Be children of the Church." After the anointing, when Elizabeth was again alone with the Sisters, she said to them: "Pity me, pray for me."[14] She took a swallow of water and remained quiet without losing consciousness.

At two o'clock after midnight on January 4, 1821, without a struggle or gasp, Elizabeth Ann Seton departed to her much-longed-for eternal home. She was laid to rest in the "sacred woods" in Saint Joseph's Valley. Fifty Sisters of Charity survived her to mourn her and to continue the work she had begun.

Today, her remains rest in the chapel of the National Shrine of Saint Elizabeth Ann Seton located in Saint Joseph's Valley, Emmitsburg, Maryland, where she lived, worked and died. She was canonized on September 14, 1975 by the late Pope Paul VI in the presence of some hundred thousand people gathered in Saint Peter's Square, Rome. She is our first native-born American saint.

In a human way, the life of Elizabeth Ann Seton foreshadowed the Second Vatican Council's description of the Holy Spirit as *the* Befriender:

> The invisible God out of the abundance of His love speaks to men as friends and lives among them so that He may invite and take them into fellowship with Himself.*

Clearly etched here, then, is the Source of Elizabeth's unique gift of friendship.

---

* *Dominum et Vivificantem*, "The Holy Spirit in the Church and the World," by Pope John Paul II; *Origins*, Vol. 16; Nov. 4, June 12, 1986. Cf. Dogmatic Constitution on Divine Revelation, 2.

CHAPTER 2

Nature Reveals God's Friendship For Me

From her earliest childhood, Elizabeth Ann Bayley Seton felt a great need for God. This chapter describes only a few of the experiences and incidents that she recalled in later life and jotted into her *Dear Remembrances* and *Diaries*. An attempt is made here to show the growth of her friendship with God and the role He played in the daily events of her life. For Elizabeth, God was everywhere. Frequently, she intermingled her love of God with her love of nature and friends. With the passage of time, God seemed to reveal Himself to her more and more in the phenomena of nature — amid her disappointments and the loss of nearly all she held dear in this world.

When Elizabeth's mother died, Betty, as she was fondly called, was told then that her mother had gone to heaven to be with God. That thought lingered with her for a long time, and she seemed never to have forgotten it. In her *Dear Remembrances*, she recalled how when she was four years old she was sitting alone on the doorstep of her home looking up to heaven in admiration of the clouds, while inside the house her little sister Catherine, two years old, lay in her coffin. When she was asked why she did not cry for Kitty, she answered that Kitty had gone up to heaven where her mama was and she wished she could go there, too.

By the time Elizabeth was six years old, her stepmother, Charlotte Amelia Barclay, had taught her the Twenty-second Psalm: "The Lord is my shepherd, the Lord ruleth me.... Though I walk in the midst of the shadow of death, I will fear no evil, for Thou art with me." This Psalm became her favorite one all through her life. During this time, Elizabeth began to teach her little half-sister, Emma, her prayers. One day, taking her up to a high window in her home, she showed her the setting sun, and told her that God lived up in heaven and good children would go there.

Between the ages of eight and twelve, while her father went to London to further his study of medicine, Elizabeth was sent to live with her uncle William Bayley on his farm in New Rochelle. There, her love of nature increased until, on one occasion, beauty met with tragedy. Her playmates took bird's eggs to destroy them. Elizabeth cried and gathered up on a leaf the young birds that were still palpitating. When she saw the mother bird hovering around and hopping from bough to bough, she hoped it would come and bring them to life. Because of this experience, she learned to walk alone when she explored nature.

In the summertime, Elizabeth was delighted to sit by the waterside or to wander for hours on the shore singing, and gathering shells or colored stones. During the winter, she would sit on the rocks surrounded with ice and sing hymns. Often, she prayed the Twenty-second Psalm that her stepmother had taught her. At times, she would sing hymns to the little children resting in their cradles. She particularly liked being with "old people" and "doing pious deeds for them."

After two years spent in New York with her father, Elizabeth, now fourteen, returned to the farm in New Rochelle while her father again continued his studies in London. During his prolonged absence, Elizabeth missed him greatly. Not hearing from him, she was afraid he might be dead. But the thought came to her that God was her Father and He would not forsake her. Desperate for some comfort from her father's supposed abandonment of her, one bright day when her cousin, Joseph Bayley, was going to the woods for brush about a mile from the farm, Elizabeth jumped into the wagon with him. While Cousin Joe cut brush, she went off into the woods and soon found an open space in a meadow. A chestnut tree with several young ones growing around it attracted her attention. When she came to it, she found rich moss under it and a warm sun. "Here then was a sweet bed," she wrote.

The still air, the clear blue vault of the sky above, the numberless sounds of spring melody and joy, the sweet clovers and wild flowers she had picked along the way, all delighted her. Her heart, as innocent as a human heart could be, was filled with enthusiastic love of God and admiration of His works.

On the farm, Elizabeth had found a comfortable spot under a favorite birch tree where she would sit and read her Bible. At times, she paused long to listen to the melody of the birds and to watch the lambs and sheep grazing on the hillside. She also delighted in musing over Milton's biblical poems and the rustic poetry of James Thomson. Walking home among the cedars, she would sing hymns and pray along the way. In the evenings, she liked to gaze at the stars, especially at the constellation Orion, the Hunter.

In her teenage loneliness, Elizabeth learned to turn to God. She was tempted to run away from home and go overseas in disguise to work for her living. But when she experienced such "folly, or sorrow, romance, miserable friendships," she turned them to good in her own heart by thinking how silly it was to love anything too much in this world. Once, when she was feeling miserable and was tempted to take an overdose of laudanum — a tincture of opium — as a means of committing suicide, she turned to God for pity and mercy. She felt that He was too good to condemn one made of dust and driven by misery, and thanked Him that He had kept her from doing that horrid deed.

In the first year of the happy marriage to William Magee Seton, Elizabeth contrasted all her blessings with other people's sufferings. The joy of having her own home at twenty awakened in her the fear that while she was enjoying her good fortune, she might lose God. But years later when she looked back on that fear while writing her memories, she felt that she did not then have a true understanding of who God was. Rather, it was her fear of hell and of being shut out from heaven that had possessed her.

As a young mother, Elizabeth had offered her children to God from their first entrance into the world. Her sweet Anna Maria she had given up a thousand times, fearing so much that the child would live only to be lost. Each of her children in their turn — William, Richard, Catherine and little Rebecca — she offered to God daily and entreated Him to take whom He pleased or all of them — if only that no one of them be lost to Him.

Yet in their new home on Long Island, as William's young wife, all nature seemed to smile at Elizabeth. There she waited for William to come home from New York three times a week — except when the moon shone; then she looked for him to come every evening. She wrote her friend, Eliza Sadler, that never before had she known such contentment as she experienced in her "little home" on the Island.

She could enjoy the pleasures of the country air without the usual interruptions.

Often her love for God blent into her love of nature. But her thoughts frequently reverted to her friends, and so often, she seemed to be looking for someone. Once, while peering at the opposite shore of the Island, bright with the setting sun, she could not help sending forth a long sigh to Eliza Sadler. Elizabeth was about two miles closer to the Narrows than Eliza and wished she could share with her the sea breeze, the mild flow of the river, the dashing of the waves, the beautiful sunset, the roses in her garden and the honeysuckles along the walk. In a later letter, she told her about the Clétera bush which "bears the sweetest flower in the greatest profusion." Its fragrance was beyond that of any wild flower she ever saw. How it would have delighted her to send Eliza a branch of it! "Like other sweets its season is passing," she wrote her, "but I will transplant a great deal of it next month. I brought home a load of it on my back."[1] How separate her love for nature from her love for friends?

Birds, too, seemed to intrigue Elizabeth. They made everything cheerful with their sweet notes. Writing to Eliza about to leave for France, Elizabeth wished her the joy of the singing of sweet birds, but not in Europe. "Come here, and hear my bird sing," she said. "It has the sweetest voice, and you may take it home and enjoy it both summer and winter." Birds seemed to set Elizabeth's mind on a happy train of thought and so she kept one in her home. One day, in a note to her sister-in-law and soul-friend, Rebecca Seton, she wrote:

> There was a young robin in a cage; its mother never left the tree it hung upon but to fetch it food, while the male flew chirping among the branches. Nelly owned it. I coaxed her to make them happy and open the cage door.

The moment she did so, out went the little one with both the old ones after it. How touching to see so much attachment among birds![2]

Like a bird herself, Elizabeth would sing the *Te Deum*, even at midnight to hush her children to sleep. Then after six hours of undisturbed sleep, with the stars disappearing and the sky a sober gray, she would awake to lie in bed for a moment in quiet joy. When she had arisen and finished her usual chores, she would stroll to the town square with her Bible in hand and enjoy two hours of sweet peace in the open air before any of her children got up. In the afternoon, however, with the sun shining brightly, she would seat her children on a rock behind the cornfield and read to them. One day, while at her father's home on Staten Island, feeling she had every advantage this world could offer to anybody, she wrote Rebecca:

> With the sun, I hope we will meet again ... it makes me think of when we will meet where our sun will never be hid. Often does the perishing body enjoy the happiness of a bright sun and every blessing surrounding it, while the soul is still imprisoned in the shades of darkness.[3]

While Elizabeth enjoyed peaceful sunsets and red clouds, as she sat on the portico of their home, she could also enjoy the disturbing drama of a rainstorm:

> A light wind rises, thunder is heard, the clouds approach and by degree cover the bright moon. Now and then the sky is lit up by lightning. At other times, the clouds pass over to Long Island and the fort is covered with a blue and spangled sky as before, while the rain beats over us.[4]

As Elizabeth became more enamored with the beauties of nature, so did she grow in her friendship with God. She once related how she sat on a little bench before the fire in her Stone Street home, her head resting in her hands, her body perfectly easy, her eyes closed and her mind serene. There she contemplated God, "the Source of all excellence and perfection." At that moment, the mortal bonds that held her soul to this world seemed to have been "gently severed, loosed more easily than untying the fastening of a fine thread without any perceptible change," she wrote.[5] That day her soul was at liberty and seemed to have fled to God and even to have possessed Him.

Nature, too, seemed to be taking on a deeper meaning for Elizabeth. To Rebecca, Elizabeth described how one evening as the clouds overspread the moon and as her father was boarding a visiting vessel, a big storm came up, but how, before her father left the vessel in a matter of less than five minutes, the storm had completely vanished leaving the sky perfectly bright again. That event seemed to symbolize a turning point in Elizabeth's philosophy of life. For, as she pondered the sudden change in the weather, her thoughts turned to the changes in her own situation in the past two years: the failure of the Seton-Maitland firm and her husband's declining health. Nature sharply symbolized these reverses.

In the very early years of her married life, she had told her friend, Eliza Sadler, that she did not resign herself to God's will without some struggle. Now, seven years later, she wrote her that she was ten thousand times more at rest than before in trusting God alone. "Come what will," she wrote, "He is above."[6]

In a lighter letter to her cherished friend, Julia Scott, she again saw nature as a symbol of her life. She asked Julia if she remembered the happy experience they had shared when in 1798, just four years after Elizabeth's marriage to William Seton, both of them had gone horseback riding along the East River to Hornbrook and had climbed the hill. They had stopped there to view the beautiful scenery stretched out below them. Elizabeth had then told Julia that this world would always be good enough for her and that she would willingly consent to remain here forever.

But only three years later, she had completely changed her view. Nothing in this world — even if all of its joys were to come to her together at one time — nothing would tempt her to live here other than God's wanting her to stay and live. "How small the world seems when one looks at it from a distance," she exclaimed, as she looked to the vast vault of the heavens.[7]

As she reflected on William's illness and financial difficulties, she wrote: "The cup that our Father has given us, shall we not drink it?" Thus, she confided to her friend, Julia Scott:

> To renounce our cherished hopes, to console ourselves with discretion when agony rends our heart, to rescue ourselves from the torpor which accompanies grief, to enter an active life even when we can find in it neither interest nor even consolation, this is proper to virtue and to the superior soul.[8]

If God so willed it, Elizabeth would "welcome sickness and pain, even shame and contempt and calumny," as she put it in her *Diaries*. Elizabeth felt that even in this world, God more than compensates us for any temporal sufferings by the possession of that peace which the world in all its beauty can neither give nor take away.

When she wrote her sister, Mary Post, Elizabeth told her that all seemed uncertain to her since her husband's illness. Again, nature seemed to speak her story to her. Whether she stood on the rocks watching the passing waves that pictured to her the passage to eternity or wandered in the woods like a pilgrim in God's world, it hardly mattered. She told her sister that the sinking sun behind the mountains reminded her of death. In heaven, however, they would find a home large enough for all of them. Their many different perspectives would be, as their husbands and friends would say, "brought to a focus," where they would behold God for all eternity.[9]

"Thy will be done" became Elizabeth's response to God's presence in her life. On Sunday, May 23, 1802, she noted in her *Diaries* that on that blessed day, her soul was first sensibly convinced of the blessing and practicability of an entire surrender of the self and of all its faculties to God. Three weeks and two days after the birth of Rebecca, her youngest child, Elizabeth had renewed her covenant of sacrificial presence with God. She had placed a seal on that covenant which she trusted would not be broken in life nor in death, in time nor in eternity, and would be noted in the Book of Life on that day.

In order to enjoy God's presence for all eternity beyond this beautiful world of nature, Elizabeth determined to serve Him with fidelity and love. She prayed:

> Lord, here am I, the creature of Thy will, rejoicing that
> thou wilt lead, thankful that Thou wilt choose for me.
> Only continue to me Thy soul-cheering presence and in
> life and in death, let me be Thy own.[10]

While travelling across the Atlantic Ocean to Leghorn, Italy, where Elizabeth, William and Anna were hoping for a milder climate for William's health, Elizabeth again shuddered, in a moment of anguish, at the thought of offending

God, of being distant to Him, as she watched the towering waves and windswept seas. Her knees trembling as they bent to Him, she renewed for the third time her mutual covenant with Him. She prayed that she might never forget that He was her *All* in and yet beyond this beautiful world.

While still at sea, Elizabeth's enthusiasm for nature was more than she dared to describe. She simply wrote Rebecca: "A quire of paper would not contain what I should tell you."[11] As she gazed at the rising and setting sun, and the moonlit evenings, she soon forgot the rocking of the vessel and the breaking of the waves. Her fatigue was lost in a refreshing sleep.

While docked in Gibraltar Bay, Elizabeth wrote Rebecca about her dream of climbing a mountain of immense height and blackness with great difficulty. As she was nearing the top almost exhausted, a voice said to her: "Never mind, take courage, there is a beautiful hill on the other side, and on it an angel waits for you." At that moment, her suffering William awakened her to help him.[12]

One morning, quarantined in the Leghorn Lazaretto, Elizabeth seemed to have forgotten herself during two hours. God's controlling presence freed her soul of its worries and gave it new life by the constant experience of His goodness. She found herself asking:

> How shall the most unwearied diligence, the most cheerful compliance, the most humble resignation, ever enough express my love, my joy, my thanksgiving and praise?[13]

Elizabeth was sure that during these two hours communing with God, she had grown ten years in her spiritual life.

When a heavy storm of lightning and thunder threatened them, she felt no fear because "the Lord on high is mightiest," she said, and He was with them. Neither did she fear the roaring of the sea, nor the heavy gale which threatened to bring down the walls of the Lazaretto. But when the sprays from the sea against the window added to William's melancholy, she cheered the bleak hours of quarantine by reliving with William many "sweet hours" by making believe she was under the chestnut tree in the meadow where cousin Joe had driven her when he went to cut brush.

During this depressing time, nature seemed to speak to Elizabeth in soothing tones. Everything around the Lazaretto seemed to be at rest except two white gulls flying to the westward toward her home and her loved ones in New York. But that thought did not satisfy her; rather the gulls were flying toward heaven where she tried to send her soul. Even the sea which had frequently been seen in violent commotion seemed to be creeping to the rocks on which it had so long been beating. Not long after this quieting of nature, William was to die and his body to be laid gently to rest in the Protestant cemetery in Leghorn.

On Elizabeth's voyage back to New York, nature seemed to speak even more eloquently to her. On April 8, 1804, the bright morning sun found her and Anna Maria, accompanied by their host and friend, Antonio Filicchi, on board the *Pyomingo*. Once embarked and underway, as they crossed the Mediterranean Sea and were nearing Spain, Elizabeth and Annina, for the whole day, watched the Pyrenees leap up from their base, "black as jade," to their dizzy summits covered with snow.

With them, Elizabeth's soul leapt up in flight toward heaven, toward the recently deceased William, as she ceaselessly repeated: "O God, Thou art my God. Here I am alone in the world with Thee and my dear little ones. But

Thou art my Father and doubly theirs."[14] The gentle motion of the sea was so calm that one could see reflected in it, as in a mirror, the white summits of the mountains colored by the sun's rays, and the moon appearing on the other coast. Within Elizabeth was this tranquil state of a soul at peace with itself, a soul faithful to God.

As they later sailed homeward through rough seas, Elizabeth peering into the ocean, meditated on the coral which at first sight is a strip of pale green. Removed from its native bed, it becomes firm, does not bend, and is almost like a rock. Its tender color then changes to a bright red. So it is with us, she thought, "submerged in the ocean of this world, subject to the vicissitudes of its waves, ready to yield under the force of each wave of temptation."[15]

On shipboard, alone with her Bible, Elizabeth spent one of the most memorable evenings of her life. The weather was mild and heavenly, reminding her of the many times she and Rebecca had stood together looking at the setting sun, sometimes with silent tears and sighs for that home where sorrow cannot enter. "Alas!" she exclaimed, "the wintry storms of time shall one day be over and the unclouded spring enjoyed forever."[16]

Even in later years, when disappointment, sorrow and tragedy continued to be her portion in life, when her soul suffered great anguish, and when, at times, God was hidden from her in her trials, Elizabeth found meaning and comfort in the beauties of nature and in her friendships. They spoke to her intimately of God. Her pilgrimage to her eternal home was a hymn of thanksgiving for all the natural beauty with which God had surrounded her. "What but the pen of an angel can ever express it?" she wrote.

Elizabeth's intimate friendship with God frequently manifested itself in her friendship with her earthly father.

CHAPTER 3

My Father
Is My First Friend

At the death of her mother when Elizabeth Ann Bayley Seton, then Betty Bayley, was still a child, her attachment for her father, Dr. Richard Bayley, deepened and he responded to her affection in the same loving manner. During her early years while she lived on her uncle William Bayley's farm at Pell House in New Rochelle, Dr. Bayley was ever faithful to his duties of caring for her welfare, despite his frequent absences for study and medical research in London, England. With her French relatives, she learned music and the French language which Dr. Bayley thought her birthright. Aware of her precocious intellect and lively disposition, he spent much of his free time sharpening her wits and quickening her imagination.

Under Dr. Bayley's tutelage during the Revolutionary period when schools were defaulting, Elizabeth learned the necessity of self-restraint, reflection and the curtailment of pleasure, qualities she carried with her throughout her life. By the time Betty was eighteen years old, she had matured to a beautiful young woman. With her marriage to William Magee Seton, an even deeper friendship developed between Elizabeth and her father which lasted until his death.

Even though preoccupied with being the first Health Officer of New York City and the founder of the Health Establishment (a dispensary and hospice) on Staten Island, Dr. Bayley nevertheless continued to shower his attention on Elizabeth. Often, he would run down in his boat to meet her at the wharf with such a welcome that it dispelled all the gloom in her heart. On one occasion his surprise visit to her and to Anna Maria so pleased her that she wrote Eliza Sadler to recount her father's remark that there never was such a pair — that he saw no such cheerful welcome expression in any other eyes in the world. Elizabeth often repeated to Eliza that her father could do no more than he was doing to prove his regret for the past absences.

In his reflections, Dr. Bayley did not seem to consider that he was indulging one of Elizabeth's most incorrigible failings — that of wanting his attention all the time. She herself knew that as a married daughter she had no right to that privilege however acceptable his unbounded generosity toward her might be. While there was a tincture of vanity in it, she could not be unaware that his attentions promoted her self-confidence. One New Year, he sent her twenty pounds of New Year cakes, honey cakes and keg biscuits to be divided between her and her half-sister, Helen, and the girls. He had also included some almonds and a box of raisins. At another time, he sent shad and two ducks.

Her father's spirit seemed to surround her. She checked each word he would oppose and pursued every action that he would approve. She rejoiced in his firmness and stability, and prayed God the Father "to treasure up the blessed Spirit, and place her in the path to attain it."[1]   In his absences she took delight in writing to him, even when there was nothing new to tell him. If he should be resting and unoccupied by his usual cares and solicites, a letter from her, she thought, would be very acceptable. If otherwise busy, he would read it in haste and the idea "Beth is a goose" would pass through his mind.

Once when she had just passed one of the most elegant evenings of her life, she wrote him that she had been reading of the "High and lofty One who inhabits Eternity" and selecting those scriptural passages that she wished to hand down to her daughter, Anna. It was then eleven o'clock and since seven she had never left her seat and scarcely changed her posture. She closed that letter with "oraisons" for her father and wished him peace.

Considering Dr. Bayley a philosopher, Elizabeth wrote him that *Monsieur* Olivier Besley, a relative and close friend, had said that she was a specimen of philosophy, "one who reasons and reflects on the consequences of actions and superior to exterior appearances, *'pas une femme savante, c'est ce que je déteste le plus.'* "[2]* Madame Besley had confided her eldest son to Elizabeth's care, a confidence Elizabeth felt flattering since Madame Besley was so particularly attentive to the morals and manners of her children. In return, Elizabeth proposed to leave her son, William, with Madame Besley the next summer as a means of his learning the French language with facility — an incalculable advantage in her eyes.

A letter to Dr. Bayley that was to have been long had to be short. *Monsieur* and Madame Besley and the family had occupied her time the previous day; her friend, Catherine Dupleix (Dué) was with her that day, and she had not done her letter-copying for William, her husband. She still had three letters to be ready for the next day's post. Of late, William had kept her busy copying mercantile correspondence in English and French and assisting him in making statements to his partner in London. That night she wrote

---

* [*"There is nothing I detest more than a female savant,"* an allusion from Moliere's play Les Femmes Savantes]

her father that one eye was open, the other shut, so she wished him a night of rest and the same for herself.

Elizabeth particularly enjoyed writing her father about her family and friends. She and William had just passed one bright late March day pleasantly together. In the morning, as they rode through the countryside breathing the pure air, they had been delighted with all the beauty surrounding them. The birds sang so loud and sweet that the season seemed six weeks more advanced. The blossoms and zephyrs of spring, the gentle but animating colors of nature — all were heightened by the conversation and smiles of "him I love." That was one side of the scene, the other she dared not look at — William's failing health.

When her father expressed concern about the family's health, Elizabeth replied that at the moment she was well, her husband better, and the children remarkable. The previous day she had been a sufferer, but the day of the letter she was cheerful and light, as if a weight had been removed. When she could walk over the floor without limping and making wry faces, she would think herself fortunate. The children were delighted with the sunshine and the promise of soon going to see "Grandpappa." The little circle saluted him. "It is impossible ever to fancy finer Grandchildren than you have," she wrote him. Little Richard Bayley, his namesake, was to be sure the center of all harmony.

Addressing Dr. Bayley as "My very dear Mr. Monitor," she wrote him that she had had the pleasure to hear a Mr. Delmas, a French physician, refer a number of strangers both French and English to a publication called the *Monitor* as containing the best thing written on the subject of yellow fever and as the only one pointing to the fever's true cause and origin. This physician had admitted that he did not know the author of the article but that the latter must be the best friend of humanity and should be considered by the

Americans as their best advisor. She then added archly that, if the prayers of a "good quiet little female" (herself) were supposed to be of any avail, they would long be continued for him with the hope that "the visual rays of our fellow citizens will in time be brightened by your labors, and their attention awakened by the voice of truth and conscience."[3]

When it was currently reported that Dr. Bayley had gone to New London to inquire about the origin of yellow fever and that he would then proceed to Boston to see his children, Elizabeth hoped that her father would very soon return. He could then convince the ladies who were chattering on the subject that the origin of the fever was not the object of his pursuit, but its remedy. The Besleys, too, had asked with great interest if the report that the Quakers had combined against the Health Officer was true. Elizabeth told her father that she explained this and a variety of reports to them as far as her information extended. Madame Besley, speaking of the present appearance of things in general observed with the finger on the side of the nose: *"Rien n'est en équilibre ni dans les physiques ni dans les morales, les têtes des hommes tournent."*[4]* Elizabeth hoped that her father's head was quiet and that his stay would be as short as possible.

During her father's extended absences, Elizabeth regretted that for his sake his visits could not be prolonged; but as for herself, the day he returned would be the most pleasant she could experience. If, at three o'clock, she should see him open the door, how her heart would dance! She told him that the vacant corner of the sofa looked melancholy, and reminded him that the faded Baltimore and Philadelphia Gazettes near the fireplace were awaiting his return. "Will not these Easterly winds bring my friend?"

---

* [*"Nothing is permanent, neither in the realm of physics, nor in morality; men change their minds."*]

she asked him. Reminiscing about their joy together one evening, she asked her father if he recollected the mild quiet evening hour when he stood in the doorway of their home on Staten Island admiring the sunset glow and observed to his Betty "all nature is hushed."

A letter from her father made her heart jump for joy; it came "like a holiday to a child that had long been kept in school and harassed by the severity of its teachers." To insure his writing her, she would put aside an hour of every day to write to him. Nothing about Dr. Bayley escaped her notice. Once when his letter arrived undated, she admonished him that he had deprived her of the small pleasure of knowing when it was written. When another letter arrived containing the news of his good health and of his expected return, the joy it brought forced Madame Besley, who had passed the day with her, to declare that her *chère fille* was *charmante* and and gave her *mille baisers*.[5]*

Life with her father on Staten Island Elizabeth considered the most interesting part of her existence. She took great satisfaction in offering him fresh bread, butter and coffee after his fatiguing sail around the Island to care for the almost countless numbers of immigrants that had arrived. Every evening after she had played for him all his favorite selections on the piano, and he had retired, she found it impossible to chase from her mind the thoughts of the severity and danger of her father's life.

Dr. Bayley never seemed to weary. Each rising sun found him already two or three hours engaged in procuring comfort for the sufferers. Except for an hour's rest at the side of Elizabeth's piano, his labors were unceasing. Elizabeth wrote their friend, Julia Scott, that her coming to the Island now would make her tremble. Just opposite the door of their dwelling there was a vessel of Irish immigrants

---

* [that her dear daughter was charming and gave her a thousand kisses]

with a hundred sick passengers to land as fast as possible. Dr. Bayley said that no one had ever seen the likes of it. Little infants were dying the moment they received fresh air, before they could be brought on shore. Many were famishing at their mother's breast unable to receive other nourishment. At that very moment, twelve children were certainly doomed to die from mere want of food.

Elizabeth tried to soothe her father. One morning, when he was busier than usual, he greeted her with a melancholy truth — that he could never rest in this world and it might as well be one thing or another. When with some displeasure he told Elizabeth that a cook was needed for the Quarantine and that he did not know how to set about getting one, she could only reply that she would write Eliza Sadler. Unwilling to overburden Eliza, she nevertheless asked her whether she could procure for them a decent woman as a cook for the Quarantine. Her wages might be anything the woman pleased, Dr. Bayley had said. And if she liked Elizabeth as the mistress of the house, she might be sure of going home to State Street in New York with her in the fall. Knowing her father's love of music, Elizabeth also asked Eliza to send on Dr. Bayley's favorite song, "Kate of Aberdeen."

For some time, Elizabeth had been uneasy about her father's health. She could not say he was well, for everyone who had had any communication with the unhappy immigrants had been more or less sick. Elizabeth wrote Eliza that she was more than thankful that her father had not been actually ill, though he had complained for several days, but never seriously. "Heaven avert that . . ." she prayed.

In the afternoon of August 10, 1801, Dr. Richard Bayley was seated at his dining room window composed, cheerful and particularly delighted as he watched the pilots maneuver the ships into the harbor. A beautiful sunset and a bright rainbow extending immediately over the bay heightened the scene. Calling Elizabeth to observe the different shades of the sun on the clover field before the door, he repeatedly exclaimed: "In my life I never saw anything so beautiful." Little Kit, Elizabeth's youngest daughter, was playing in her arms while Dr. Bayley amused himself with spooning the child some tea from his glass and making her say "Papa." After tea, Elizabeth played all her father's favorite tunes. He sang two German hymns and, ironically, "The Soldier's Adieu" with such earnestness and energy that even the servants observed how much more cheerful he was that evening than on any other evening during the summer. At ten o'clock, an hour later than usual, he went to bed.

The next morning, his breakfast was ready at just about sunrise. His servant reported to Elizabeth that her father had been out since daylight and had returned home sick. He took his cup of tea in silence as he was accustomed to do, then went to the wharf and visited the sick in the surrounding buildings. When Elizabeth saw him shortly afterwards, he was sitting on a log exposed to the hottest sun of the summer. His distressed look threw her immediately into tears. An umbrella was sent out to him for his protection against the beating sun. When he came back into the house sometime later, he told her that his legs had given way under him. He then went to bed and became immediately delirious.

During his week-long illness, neither opium nor any remedy whatever could give him a moment's relief. Blister upon blister produced no change for the better; everything he took his stomach rejected with continual dreadful retchings. Nor could he lie still in his bed unless constantly holding Elizabeth's hand. In a hurried note to her sister-in-law, she wrote: "Oh, my Rebecca, if I did not in this hour know who to look to, how could it be borne? Your heart suffers on my account, but alas, it suffers in vain. The chance of saving him is so slim."[6] Little Kit, the baby, was very good and allowed Elizabeth to pass the greater part of the night in her father's room. Though very seldom nursed in three days, she had never whimpered.

The third day, Dr. Bayley looked earnestly into Elizabeth's face and said: "The hand of heaven is in all this: nothing more can be done." He complained that it was hard work, and repeatedly called, "My Christ Jesus, have mercy on me."[7] With these words, Elizabeth was comforted that his salvation was secured. Except for two hours that night both Elizabeth and her sister, Mary Post, were with him. The next day, Elizabeth's two older children, Anna and William, went to stay with Mary Post. Dr. Wright Post, Mary's husband, sat up with him one night. The next morning he went to town and returned with Dr. Tillary who would stay with Dr. Bayley until the situation changed.

Any moment that Elizabeth was away, her father would miss her and send for her. "Come sit by me," he would say. "I have not rested a minute since you left me. Cover me warm. I have covered many poor little children. I would cover you more, but it can't always be as we would wish. All the horrors are coming, my child, I feel them all."[8] These expressions and the charge he gave Elizabeth of his keys convinced her that he knew the worst from the beginning.

The night before Dr. Bayley died, Kit lay all night in a fever at Elizabeth's breast and Richard on his mattress at her feet was vomiting violently. Elizabeth wrote Rebecca: "The Father in heaven is the only solace left to your sister. He never withdraws Himself. Oh, how sweet is such a solace at this time."[9] On the day of Dr. Bayley's death, August 17, 1801, he struggled in extreme pain from one o'clock of this Monday afternoon until about half-past two. When it became apparent that he was resting easily, he put his hand in

Elizabeth's, turned on his side and breathed out the last of life without a groan or appearance of pain.

In the interval of his interment, Elizabeth saw her father's composed, quiet countenance several times. Doctor Bayley was finally buried on Staten Island in Saint Andrew's Churchyard in Richmond, close to the church on the east side. Because the parish of Richmond had refused to have his remains carried through the Island, the grave was at first dug in a corner near the house where Elizabeth's children were accustomed to play. "But as if the mercy of my heavenly Father directed it," Elizabeth wrote Julia Scott, "we thought of taking him in his barge to Richmond which could go within half a mile of the Churchyard, where he was at last laid by young Dr. Joseph Bayley [her father's associate], and his faithful boatmen. The sexton nor none of the people dared to approach."[10] Dr. Channing Moore of the Island performed the burial service and two wagons full of relatives and friends paid the last respects.

In a heart-rending note to Dr. Moore, Elizabeth expressed her gratitude for his services and her deep love for her father. It read:

> I cannot leave the Island without offering to Mr. Moore the acknowledgments of a grateful heart for the blessing and comfort he has procured for us in the bitter hours of heavy affliction. You have, dear Sir, placed the remains of my dear Father in a sacred resting place, and the only remaining wish I have is that a small space may be reserved on each side of him for his two eldest children. This request is not the impulse of unrestrained sorrow, but of a heart that knows where its Home is to be and feels the greatest consolation in the Hope that it may be permitted to repose by its dear Parent.[11]

MY FATHER IS MY FIRST FRIEND

In her letter to Julia Scott written on September 5, 1801, several weeks after her father's death, Elizabeth poured out her heart:

> I, his dear, his darling child, whose soul doated [sic] on him, without perceptible struggle, and with the calmness of a subdued spirit, after once the soul was departed, saw all, did all that was to be done, and now review with wonder and grateful praise that I live much less that I have lived through it.[12]

The gravestone which Elizabeth Ann Seton noted in her *Diaries* is on a white marble tablet raised a few feet from the ground above her father's grave.

In Memory of
DOCTOR RICHARD BAYLEY OF NEW YORK
Who after practicing the various branches of his profession
with unwearied diligence and High Reputation
for 30 years in that City
Projected a plan, and for five years conducted the operations
of a Lazaretto on this island.
Intelligent in divising, and indifatigable [sic] in pursuing
Plans subservient to the cause of Humanity
He continued to guard the Public Health with persevering industry
And in the midst of dangers to perform with Invincible fortitude
the Hazardous duties of Health Officer
Until in the discharge of this Important trust
He was siezed [sic] with a Malignant fever
To which he fell a lamented Victim
And thus terminated a life of great usefulness
on the 17th August 1801
Aged 56 years.

For Elizabeth Seton her father was not dead. "His spirit is ever with his own darling," she wrote Eliza Sadler. Two years after Dr. Bayley's death, Elizabeth had an unlooked-for enjoyment. She walked through the Quarantine garden and trod every wharf-plank on which her father's feet had walked. She had sailed over the Bay in his boat with Darby at the sail and with William, her husband, at the helm. As they reminisced, Darby commented that he would never meet such a friend again. He was the poor man's friend. William, too, paid him a tribute, saying that Dr. Bayley was the best friend he ever had. He also recounted that when he had got out of his sickbed on the day before Dr. Bayley's illness to row him for the last time round the Island, Dr. Bayley had remarked that it was too much for William. But William had answered: "Never mind if the row is too much for me."[13] Elizabeth later spent an hour with her father's successor, Dr. Joseph Bayley, at the Quarantine in her father's room on the very spot where she last stood during his illness.

Elizabeth's love for her father lived on in her happy memories of him and in his work now carried on by his friends. His memory was ever warm in her heart when instructing her children in the principles he had inculcated in her. Having been separated from him in this world, she looked to the happy reunion that awaited them in the next where her loves for him and the Heavenly Father would become one. This tragic event in her life strengthened her trust in God alone — a trust which became her secret strength in bearing the sorrows lying ahead.

CHAPTER 4

WILLIAM MAGEE SETON
My Husband And Friend

Little did Betty Bayley dream that her first meeting with William Magee Seton at a ball held in the De Lancey home for the elite in New York City would lead to marriage. It was not long after, however, that she began having serious thoughts about him. Soon they began to meet each other in the homes of friends according to the custom of the time.

When their mutual friend, Eliza Sadler, was not going to the concert and wished very much to see them, Elizabeth would write William urging him not to be too late. Once when Mrs. Sadler was invited to drink tea with Mrs. Constable, Elizabeth wrote William that if he was anxious to see her, he would find her playing the piano at Mrs. Atkinson's. On still another occasion, Elizabeth let William know that she intended to pass an hour in the evening with Mrs. Wilkes where he might have the honor of seeing her, if it pleased him. One evening, when Elizabeth's infected eye ("very ugly" but not "very painful") had prevented her leaving the house, she wrote William that Doctor Wright Post, her brother-in-law, was going out of town that day and that the family was dining at one o'clock. She wanted him to come as early as possible so that he could devote a great deal of his time to her. In a second note, she told him that she was well and would be perfectly happy if she could enjoy his company.

One day when Dr. Bayley, her father, had earlier dined with the family without her knowing when or where he was later going, she estimated that William would not be able to meet him until the evening. Interested in her father's good opinion of William, she wrote William that she had already made the apology for his afternoon absence. That same day, she planned to meet him at five o'clock on Wall Street and would tell him more about the meeting with her father.

After a fitting courtship, Elizabeth and William were united in marriage at the home of her sister and brother-in-law, Dr. and Mrs. Wright Post. The Episcopalian minister, Bishop John Provoost of New York City, officiated at the ceremony.

Elizabeth was happy with William in their home at 27 Wall Street and wrote a friend: "My own home at 20 [years old] — that and heaven, too, quite impossible." At that moment, William was playing "Rosy Dimpled Boy," "Pauvre Madelon," "Return Enraptured Hours" and "Carmignol" in rotation as fast as his Stradivarius could sound them. She had not yet opened the box of music Eliza Sadler had sent, but she wrote her that she would learn it with very little difficulty, as simplicity was Eliza's taste. In a later letter to her sister-in-law, Rebecca Seton, Elizabeth described an evening of happiness with William; the cheerful fire was blazing and a bright moon was shining over her shoulder. Overjoyed by her Willy's appearance and good spirits that week, she added: "Willy's please must be my please."[1]

One afternoon when she had gone for a walk on the Fort with Willy swinging the spy glass, all the scenes wore a smile and Elizabeth considered that day as happy a day for her as a mortal ought to have. Once when Willy said he would dine at home, she wrote Rebecca that she should be only too happy, provided he kept his promise freely without any persuasion from her.

Away from home or at any time without William, Elizabeth was far from contented. She passed one Christmas day with her father and sister, Mary Post, leaving William at home with the children. She had promised to go and nothing could persuade William to let her stay at home. She wrote Rebecca that she went feeling "like a wretch."

Then, one summer while she and the children were on Staten Island with her father and William was working in New York, William told her she must not come home to New York until October. Elizabeth was tired of meeting him but once a week and finding him wearied and out of spirits. She considered this a "strange way of living." She wrote William that the children were as merry as birds. They did not understand that their "Papa was not to come nor tomorrow, nor the next day, nor the day after. That is for their mother to feel."[2] When William next came to the Island and spent three consecutive days with them, Elizabeth's joy was such that she played the piano more during that time than in the whole previous year.

Very early in their marriage, however, William's health became a source of concern for Elizabeth. She wrote their friend, Eliza Sadler, that on William's health depended their every hope of human happiness. If it did not mend, it would sink her in the "lowest depth of sorrow."[3] On one occasion when William needed release from his business affairs to restore his health, Elizabeth sent him some forgotten items and included a note: "My love, . . . Is it possible that I am not to see you again for so long a time? Heaven protect you and return you again in safety!"[4] During these attacks of illness and fatigue, Elizabeth felt that William's heart grew every day more tender. She wrote Rebecca: "If you had known how sweet last evening was — Willy's heart seemed to be nearer to me for being nearer to His God."[5]

About this time, the yellow fever epidemic broke out in New York and Elizabeth's concerns about William's health increased. He went every day to town. Even when he was quite sick with a pain in his side and was more exposed than many who had already been stricken, the cabriolet came for him because the banks had to be attended and the bills paid. Elizabeth felt that William's escape from ill-health depended on the mercy of God which had never yet failed her. She wrote Rebecca that if William did not survive, the greatest probability was that she and Rebecca would never meet again for she "could never survive the scene." The happy evenings she had imagined: the music, the readings, must all be given to the winds, she felt, for she would no longer indulge expectations at the mercy of chance.

To add to their plight, only four years after their marriage, William's father, William Seton Sr., slipped on the front steps of their home and died from the fall. This left William and Elizabeth to assume the responsibility of a large family and the international mercantile interests of the Seton-Maitland shipping firm. For herself, Elizabeth feared nothing, but trembled at the heavy load these obligations put on William's spirits. He soon became anxious and, when Elizabeth talked to him about "hope," he answered that he was "too much troubled." She wrote Rebecca that God alone could set him right and that hope must go on with them, for it would not do for hearts and fortunes to sink together.[6]

Elizabeth tried to keep the Seton-Maitland affair to herself and not to disturb Rebecca's mind with the truth of William's misfortune. But when Rebecca reproached Elizabeth for dissembling with her, Elizabeth admitted that Mr. James Maitland, William's and Rebecca's brother-in-law, had stopped payment on goods in London, and that upon the general decisions of his friends and the Directors of the Banks, William was obliged to do the same in New York. Elizabeth wrote Rebecca:

> It is a cruel event to William for altho' he has every consolation a man can have under such circumstances, that it is not from his own imprudence, and that no part of the blame is attached to him. You may imagine the distress and perplexity it occasions to all [of us].[7]

At times, William said he would work it out; at others, he felt that nothing remained for him but State Prison and poverty. He could not know with certainty how it would go until Maitland had arranged finally with his creditors in London and in Hamburg.

At first, William's hopes were kept up at the idea that Mr. Maitland's next letter would explain the situation of his affairs, and the Setons would then know what to expect. But on the contrary, Mr. Maitland wrote that the creditors had attached claim to *all* the property and that his mind was in such a state that he could say no more. Vessel after vessel arrived and correspondents in London and Hamburg notified William that his bills were refused and his property detained there. Yet not one line of explanation, either good or bad, came from Maitland.

Meanwhile, the wearied William did not know if he had enough money to buy bread for his family. Obliged to transfer his possessions in trust to his friends, William was willing to give up everything, even his furniture, in order to be free of "these everlasting struggles." Already, there was one lawsuit against him. This gave reason to expect more.

During these hard times, Elizabeth dared not talk to William about money. On one occasion when he asked her to enclose ten dollars to Eliza Sadler for the baker and the milkman, she asked him for the money, but he did not have it. She later wrote Rebecca: "This morning's sun found me without a penny; it is now setting and we are worth twenty dollars in possession and the Ladies [of Charity] have to refund me ten dollars. Tomorrow then we shall have thirty dollars, delightful."[8] Elizabeth felt that patience was the only choice and that to think about the affair was all in vain, but her hope in God never wavered.

While daily expecting the arrival of her third child, Elizabeth had to keep up not only her own courage but William's as well. To see William come home heated, wearied and covered with dust and to hear his reflections on what was to become of his wife and children (besides the large family of Setons left in his charge) was, indeed, discouraging to Elizabeth. Both of them had so much to fear that it was terrible to think of. But Elizabeth wrote Rebecca, "When things are at their worst, they must grow better."[9] For one entire week, Elizabeth and William wrote letters to their clients until one and two o'clock in the morning. William never closed his eyes until daylight and then for not more than an hour. Elizabeth could hardly make time for the necessary work which fell to her as mother and housekeeper. She told Rebecca that she would rather have a great deal to do than not, for then it would be sooner done. As time went on and William had arranged the statement of his accounts as much as he could, his mind became more composed, but his health did not improve.

Elizabeth made her husband's trials her own. When the doctors recommended a sea voyage to restore her husband's failing health, Elizabeth determined to accompany him to Leghorn, Italy, as guests of his business partners and friends, Antonio and Filippo Filicchi. The voyage would take fifty-six days. Despite the objections of their New York relatives and friends who accused Elizabeth of folly next to madness, the Setons planned to set sail on the *Shepherdess* leaving New York Harbor on October 2, 1803. Meanwhile, Elizabeth had arranged to leave her children in the care of her sister, Mary Post, and her sister-in-law, Rebecca Seton.

As the ship was rounding the lighthouse at the outlet of New York Bay, Elizabeth addressed a few lines to Rebecca Seton. She told her that William felt the passing of the Battery so much that she could scarcely wave her handkerchief, but, since then, William had been very composed and better than on shore. The Bible and her cross were her source of peace and comfort. When a storm threatened, she looked neither behind nor before, only up. "He [the Lord] is with me, what can I fear?" she exclaimed.[10]

At sea, on October 28, 1803, when they had passed the Western Islands half-way between New York and Leghorn and were expecting to meet some vessel that might take her letters to New York, Elizabeth wrote Rebecca that William was daily growing better. One subject she wanted to share with Rebecca — "the dear, the tender, the gracious love with which every moment" had been marked in her heavy hours of trial. With Christ as her rock, she had not a despondent thought to contend with.

On November 18, 1803, after a voyage of seven weeks, the *Shepherdess* dropped anchor at the pier in Leghorn, just as the bells pealed forth the *Ave Maria*. The *Shepherdess* was the first ship to bring the news of the yellow fever epidemic in New York City. On hearing this, the port authorities in Leghorn forbade the passengers to disembark without a bill of health. Because of William's illness, the Setons were detained on board ship to be confined to a prison-like Lazaretto some miles off shore. They were to be quarantined for at least a month. When Elizabeth heard this, her joy turned to consternation and dismay as she looked at William in his weakened condition.

The Filicchi brothers, Antonio and Filippo, with Guy Carleton Bayley, Elizabeth's half-brother, waited for them at the wharf and were likewise disappointed. Ironically, at that moment, the band of music that welcomed strangers came under the Setons' cabin windows and played "Hail Columbia" and all those little tunes that set their children singing and dancing at home. Mr. O'Brien, the ship's captain and the rest were wild with joy, but Elizabeth hid in her berth, her heart full of sorrow and ready to break as she gazed on William who looked as if he would not live out the day.

Soon a boat with fourteen oars appeared. Hurried into the boat with only one change of clothes, the Setons were promised that the rest of their belongings would be brought on Monday. Then they were towed out to sea again. After an hour's ride over the waves, they approached the chains across the entrance of the canal which led to the Lazaretto. At the signal of a succession of bells, the chains were let down. After another bit of rowing between high walls and amidst "the quarreling and hallooing of the waterman" as to where they should be landed, the boat stopped. An hour later after much consultation and whispering with his Lieutenant, "Monsieur le Capitaine" told the Setons they might come out. Elizabeth, disheartened, wrote Rebecca that as they did so, everyone retreated from them. A guard pointed with his bayonet the way they were to go. The order sent from the Commandant of their boat to the Capitano was received on the end of a stick. Before it could be read, a fire was lighted to smoke it.

Elizabeth's carefully packed books, the papers in the little secretary, and the mattresses brought over from the ship were all examined minutely. The guard who performed this duty was subject to the same quarantine as the Setons. William tottered along as if every minute he might fall. If this had happened, no one would have dared for life to touch him. The Setons were directed to go to the window of the Capitano's house where Mrs. Filippo Filicchi, the former Mary Cowper of Boston, sat waiting to greet them with "compliments and kind looks." Elizabeth feared, however, that the fence between them did not hide her fatigue of soul and body.

Shortly, Elizabeth and William were shown the door they should enter, No. 6, up twenty stone steps to a room with high arched ceilings, brick floor, and naked walls. With little delay, William's mattress was spread out on the cold floor and he upon it. Elizabeth had heard that the Lazaretto was the very place of comfort for the sick and had left on board ship their little syrups, currant jelly and drinks which William must take every half hour. Meanwhile the Capitano had sent them three warm eggs, a bottle of wine and some pieces of bread, but William could touch neither the wine nor the eggs. Elizabeth finding a tiny room in which she could rest her weakened knees wrote Rebecca that there she "emptied her heart and washed the bricks with her tears," then returned to William.

At sunset, when the kind Filicchis came with dinner and other necessities for them, the Setons went again to the grate to speak to them. Not long after that, William fell sound asleep on the shipmattress. He had just had a fit of coughing and brought up blood. This had distressed him despite all his attempts to hide it. Elizabeth trusted that God who had given him strength to go through a day of such exertion would carry them both through this heavy trial. She wrote Rebecca that her eyes smarted so much with crying, wind and fatigue that she must close them and lift up her heart, but sleep did not come easily. She continued:

If the wind, (for it was said there were never such storms as that season) that almost put out my candle and blew on my William through the crevices and over our chimney like loud thunder could come from any but His command, or if the circumstances that have placed us in so forlorn a situation were not guided by His hand, miserable indeed would be our case.[11]

At ten o'clock that night, Elizabeth sat in one corner of the immense Lazaretto, locked in and barred with as much ceremony as any criminal might be. Nevertheless she wrote in her journal for Rebecca's sake and not without humor, the above account of the day's events. Rebecca could not rest in her bed, Elizabeth penned, if she could see her as she was then — in a room "with a single window double-grated with iron through which, if she should want anything she was to call a sentinel with a fierce cocked hat and a long rifle gun — that is, that he may not receive the dreadful infection they were supposed to have brought from New York."[12]

The next morning was Sunday. Elizabeth was awakened by the matin bells with the most painful regrets that she could not find relief even in prayer. From the little room in their apartment, she viewed the open sea and watched the beating of the waves against the high rocks at the entrance of the Lazaretto. The rocks threw the waves violently back and raised the white foam as high as the Lazaretto's walls. Reflecting on how dark thoughts were shutting out her only consolation, her husband and her God, she turned to William with a smile and asked what they should do for breakfast. Filippo, the guard, had unbarred the doors and placed a bottle of milk near the entrance of the room. William took some milk with bread, while Elizabeth walked the floor with a crust and a glass of wine. William's pain was so severe that he could not sit up.

Elizabeth watched him on the cold bricks unwarmed by a fire, shivering, groaning, lifting his chin to set his sorrowful eyes on her face with tears running down on his pillow. While he uttered not a word, she rubbed his hands until the fever came on, and then she suffered with him.

That day the Capitano brought them news that their time in the Lazaretto was lessened five days. When he told Elizabeth to be satisfied with the dispensations of God, she answered him with such a succession of sobs that he soon departed. Later, Mr. Filicchi came to comfort William. He had brought dinner from town and a man-servant to stay with them during their quarantine. Elizabeth described the servant thus to Rebecca, "Louis, an old man, very little, [with] gray hairs, and blue eyes which changed their expression from joy to sorrow, as if they would console and still enliven."[13] Tired of the sight of men with cocked hats, cockades, and bayonets, she had covered her face with a handkerchief, and did not look up when Louis first came into their apartment. When she refused the dinner, he prayed with uplifted hands that God would comfort her. Touched by his compassion, she wrote Rebecca that she would long remember his voice of sorrow and tenderness.

Having entered the quarters occupied by the Setons and touched what they had touched, Louis soon became an object of equal terror. The bolts of the adjoining door were hammered open and he was given the next room. Elizabeth wrote Rebecca, "How many times did the poor man run up and down the nearly perpendicular twenty steps to get things necessary for our comfort the next morning."[14] It seemed to Elizabeth that opening her prayer book and bending her knees was the signal for her soul to find rest. After prayers together, William soon fell asleep. Elizabeth read her little book of sermons and became more happy than she had been wretched. That night she went to bed at twelve, rose twice to pray and to help her "poor William."

The next morning, Monday, Elizabeth gave William his warm milk. Then, as usual, she applied herself to reading the Scriptures and began to consider their situation as one of the steps in the dispensation of God's will which, she felt, could alone choose right for them. When the Capitano came with his guards, they put up a very neat bed and the curtains sent by the Filicchis. They also arranged a couch for Elizabeth to lie down upon, and wrote their names on a bill of delivery. The Capitano's voice of kindness again entreated her to look up to *"le bon Dieu"* and made her regard the speaker. Elizabeth told Rebecca that she saw in him every expression of a benevolent heart. His great cocked hat being off, she found that it had hidden his gray hairs and a kind and affectionate countenance. Clasping his hands, he looked up, and then at William, saying: "If God calls, what can we do?" With that she began to like her Capitano.[15]

As Elizabeth looked around their prison, she found its situation was not without a touch of beauty. She comforted William all she could by "rubbing his hands, and wiping his tears, and giving words to his soul which was too weak to pray for itself."[16] That evening, as she watched the setting sun in the midst of a cloud she prayed, wept and then continued praying until eleven o'clock. It was not difficult to know the time of day and night in the Lazaretto. Four bells struck every hour and one bell rang out every quarter of an hour.

The next day, Mr. Filicchi accompanied by Dr. Tutilli paid the Setons a visit. William seemed better and was encouraged by Dr. Tutilli's kind words. The Setons talked with them at the grate below their room. With great difficulty, Elizabeth helped William back up the stairs, cared for him, read to him and made the best of their troubles. Louis, their servant, brought an elegant bouquet of jasmine, geraniums and pinks. He made excellent soup and cooked all with charcoal in little earthen pots. The Capitano again brought them news that another five days were granted and on the nineteenth of December they would be free. William with a blanket over his shoulders would sometimes creep to the "old man's fire." Elizabeth passed that evening quite reconciled to the sentinel's watch and bolts and bars. Despite the heavy gale, she was not afraid to put her candle at the window; the shutter was the only piece of wood about them. At this juncture, Elizabeth was not only willing to take her cross but kissed it too, just as William had an attack seemingly beyond his strength.

Elizabeth felt that every moment not spent in prayer, reading the Bible and nursing William was a loss. Her confinement of body paradoxically gave her a new liberty of soul. When she was fatigued and could no longer look up with cheerfulness, she would hide her head on the chair by William's bedside. He thought she was praying; and pray she did. "Without it, I would be of little service to him," she wrote Rebecca. Then one day, one of those sweet pauses in spirit when the body seems to be forgotten, came over her. She reminisced about that unforgettable morning in May 1789, when she had jumped in the wagon with her cousin Joe and, while Joe cut the brush, she found a chestnut tree surrounded by young ones with its seat of warm moss.

Elizabeth wrote Rebecca that all this came strong in her head that morning when the body had left the spirit alone. She had cried heartily for strength as she had done daily, even hourly, when she looked at William. With her head on the table, she had closed her eyes and lived those sweet hours over again making believe she was under the chestnut tree. Then turning to William, she found her heart peaceable, full of love for God, and confidently hoping in Him.

Frequently, Elizabeth and William conducted a prayer-service together, Elizabeth at his bedside calling herself the "preacher." Often when William heard Elizabeth repeat the Psalms of triumph in God and listened to her reading Saint Paul's faith in Christ with her whole soul, this so enlivened his spirit that he made them his own. Elizabeth began to feel that the hours she had spent reading King David and the Prophet Isaiah would always appear to her as the most precious. They seemed to turn sorrow into joy. When on one occasion, William read the last chapter of Revelation, Elizabeth wrote Rebecca that "the tone of his voice no heart could stand." At sunset they were called to prayer by the ringing of the *Ave Maria* bell, and later by the *De Profundis*, the bells "for the dead" which continued a long while and called them again in the morning to prayer for the "Souls in Purgatory."

Elizabeth and William not only prayed together but, at times, cried together. Elizabeth lamented not having any syrup or cough softener to ease William's throat. All she could offer him from day to day was milk and bark, Iceland moss and opium pills which he took quietly as a duty, without seeming even to hope that his health might improve. He had often told Elizabeth that it was too late; his strength was failing every hour and that it would not be long before he should be gone. His only hope was in Christ. "What other hope do we need?" whispered Elizabeth. Sometimes, she could inspire him for a few minutes to feel that it would be sweet to die. Often she would say to him:

> When you awake in that World, you will find nothing could tempt you to return to this; you will see that your care over your wife and little ones was like a hand only to hold the cup which God himself will give if He takes you.[17]

William always answered her: "My Father and my God, thy will be done." Elizabeth assured him that it was not from the impulse of terror that he turned to God. Long before this trial, he tried to serve Him. "When the soul is on the brink of departure, it must cling to God with increased force or where is it?" she queried.[18] On their son William's birthday, Elizabeth ventured to remind her husband of it, but he was so weak that even a thought of home and children made him shed tears. Elizabeth found that her attempt to cheer him up was useless. It seemed to her that he felt easier after venting his sorrow. That day, the Capitano said a great deal on the pleasure they would have seeing the ceremonies at the Christmas celebration in Pisa. "The enjoyment of Christmas!" Elizabeth exclaimed, her thoughts reverting to their "little ones" in New York where she would be with them in spirit.

In their sorrow, the Setons were not without friends. When Captain O'Brien's mate came to visit them, he was accompanied by one of the sailors who was "always flying to serve them and trying to please them while on board ship." Elizabeth talked to them out of the grated window. Charles Bayley, who had lived with the Setons on Staten Island, was also with them. Seeing Elizabeth's head out of the iron bars, he called out, "Mrs. Seton, are you in prison?" As he was leaving, he looked behind him all the way until he could no longer see her. Speaking of the attentive sailor, Elizabeth wrote Rebecca, "I shall never hear a sailor's yo, yo without thinking of his melancholy song. He is the Captain's and everybody's favorite."[19]

A few days later, Captain O'Brien and his wife also found their way to the Setons. Filippo, the guard, divided them with his stick saying, "Must not touch, Signora." While William peeped through the grates, Elizabeth ran down the steps to meet the O'Briens. Mrs. O'Brien began to sob and the kind, affectionate Captain had tears in his eyes. Because of the cold, the Setons could see them only a few minutes. In an effort to heat their apartment, the Lazaretto Capitano had sent them hand irons, small wood and coal. To make the smoke bearable, Elizabeth decked the chimney with a curtain. She wrote Rebecca, "How often have we nursed the fire together as I do now *alone; alone*, recall the word." She was surrounded by her Bible, the *Commentary on the Book of Psalms* and the *Following of Christ*. "The company is numberless," she exclaimed.[20]

About two weeks before the Setons were to leave the Lazaretto, Elizabeth was awakened by William in great suffering. Noticing the serious change in him, Elizabeth immediately sent for Dr. Tutilli. When he saw William in his dying condition, he told Elizabeth that he was not the one needed, but that she must send "for him who would minister to his soul." At that moment, Elizabeth felt that she stood alone, she wrote Rebecca. William and Elizabeth looked in silent agony at each other, each fearing to weaken the other's strength. Drawing himself toward her, he said, "I breathe out my soul with you." The exertion caused him to throw a quantity from his lungs. In so doing, a few hours later, he seemed "nearly the same as when first they entered the Lazaretto."

Elizabeth spent that day close by William's bedside on her little mat. While William slumbered the most of every hour, Elizabeth prayed. No breakfast or dinner interrupted his rest and for some time, no enquiring visitor disturbed the solemn silence. At sunset, Guy Carleton, Elizabeth's half-brother, came to pay them a visit. The Capitano, too, offered much kindness. He was shocked at William's stillness and distressed at the thought that Elizabeth was alone with him. Dr. Tutilli had told him that despite his present relief, if the expectoration from the lungs did not return, he might be gone in a few hours. When the Capitano asked Elizabeth if she would like someone in the room with her, she answered him, "Oh, no, what have I to fear?" "And what had I to fear?" she reiterated in her letter to Rebecca. She lay down most of the day, as if to rest, so that William might not be uneasy.

All night, Elizabeth listened; sometimes by the fire, sometimes lying on her couch. At times, she thought his breathing had stopped; at others, she was alarmed by its heaviness. To feel if his face was cold, she would kiss him. Not the smallest murmur did he utter. Reduced almost to nothing, the lifting of his eyes was the strongest expression she had yet seen in his rapid decline. Elizabeth wrote Rebecca that from its very nature, his complaint had given him no release from irritation in sudden violent coughing, chills, oppressions or weakness. Even the weight of his own limbs seemed more than he could bear. "Why are thou so heavy, my soul?" was the only comfort he seemed to find in words. While praying for William, Elizabeth experienced wonder to think that God could and would hear her through the most severe trials. Asking herself the question, "Well, was I alone?", her answer came in the next breath: "Dear indulgent Father, could I be alone, while clinging fast to Thee in continual prayers of thanksgiving?"[21]

At daylight, William seemed somewhat better. The Reverend Mr. Thomas Hall, the Protestant minister, came in the morning with Mr. Filicchi and the Capitano. When they left, they said they would come back again. Elizabeth wrote Rebecca:

> No one ever saw my William without giving him the qualities of an amiable man. But to see the character exalted to the peaceful humble Christian waiting the will of God with a patience that seems more than human, and

a firm faith which would do honor to the most distinguished piety, is a happiness allowed only to the poor little mother [herself] who is separated from all other happiness connected with this scene of things.[22]

Elizabeth considered it her exclusive privilege to serve Christ in William's soul and body. To console and soothe him in those hours of affliction, pain, watching and weariness, she felt that she alone could do it next to God. To her presence, William attributed the cheerful notes of hope and Christian triumph that he enjoyed, calling her "his life, his soul, his dearest, his all." He declared that it was she who first taught him to pronounce the name of Jesus and to love the sweetness of its sound. Except for the day they had thought his last, William never failed to join Elizabeth in prayer since they had entered the Lazaretto. She wrote Rebecca:

> Oh, if I were in the dungeon of this Lazaretto, I should bless and praise my God for these days of retirement and abstraction from the world which have afforded leisure and opportunity for so blessed a work.[23]

When Elizabeth thanked God that night for creating her and preserving her, it was with a warmth of feeling she had never known until that moment.

During the remaining days of their quarantine, William reminiscing, often said that this was the period of his life which, if he lived or died, he would always consider as "blessed, the only time he had not lost." He spoke of his children and of meeting his family in heaven, of the friends he had left behind, as if it were but yesterday. He thought of the Reverend Mr. Henry Hobart (the Episcopalian minister at Trinity Church in New York City) whose visits and society he missed most, his strongest consolation in these hours of sorrow. That day, Elizabeth said her prayers alone, while William was asleep; she did not dare to remind him of them; weakness and pain had quite overpowered him. When the Capitano entered the room and looked up to heaven, Elizabeth vented her feelings:

> Well, I know that God is above, Capitano, you need not always point your silent look and finger there; if I thought our condition the providence of man, instead of the "weeping Magdalene" as you so graciously call me, you would find me a lioness, willing to burn your Lazaretto about your ears, if it was possible that I might carry off my poor prisoner to breathe the air of heaven in some seasonable place.[24]

> To keep a poor soul, who comes to your country for his health thirty days shut up in damp walls, smoke and wind from all corners, blowing even the curtain round his bed (and his bones almost through) and now the shadow of death trembling, if he only stands a few minutes![25]

The prospects of his going to Pisa for his health seemed very distant that day.

By the end of their stay in the Lazaretto, Elizabeth had completely finished reading the New Testament which she had begun on the sixth of October while at sea. Her Bible, she had read to herself in sequence as far as Ezekiel. The passages in Isaiah that she had just finished reading to William, he enjoyed so much that he was carried for awhile beyond his troubles. Reflecting on the Scripture readings as the law of God and considering them sacred, he told Elizabeth that he felt like a person brought to the light after many years of darkness. The Friday night before the Setons were to move from the Lazaretto to Pisa, they were bolted into their apartment, for the authorities expected to find William dead the next day. But he rested quietly that night and "God is with us," Elizabeth wrote Rebecca. Over the weekend, she kept up his courage and hope by picturing to him their removal to Pisa.

On Monday morning, December 19, Elizabeth arose with the dawn and had everything ready for their departure by ten o'clock. The Setons waited anxiously for the arrival of the Filicchis' coach which was to conduct them at eleven o'clock that morning to Pisa, on the border of the Arno River, where the Filicchis had engaged for them new quarters. While William was seated on the arms of two men who carried him from the Lazaretto to the coach, Elizabeth held his hand. A multitude of gazers, surrounding them sighed out, *"O Pauverino"* [sic]. Elizabeth's heart beat almost to fainting lest William should die in the exertion. But the air revived him; his spirits were cheerful, and through fifteen miles of heavy roads supported by pillows and cordials, he appeared stronger than when they set out. "My Father and my God!" was all Elizabeth's thankful heart could utter.

The next day in Pisa, before jotting any notes in her Journal to Rebecca, Elizabeth stopped and asked herself if she could go through the remainder of her "memorandum" with the same sincerity and exactness as in the past. She questioned, too, whether in the many anxieties and sorrows she would endure in the little time allotted to William, she could suppress the overflowing of her feelings and "her soul stand singly before God." The answer came quickly, "Yes, every moment of it speaks His praise and therefore it shall be followed."[26]

Elizabeth then wrote Rebecca that William was composed the greater part of the day on the sofa. Delighted with his change of situation, the taste and elegance of everything around him, he enjoyed fully every necessary comfort within his reach. Together they read, compared the past and the present, talked of heavenly hopes with Guy Carleton who had come to stay with them. Both William and Elizabeth had retired in hopes of a good night, but Elizabeth had scarcely fixed the pillows of the sofa which she was to make her bed, when William called her to help him. From that moment the last complaint, which Dr. Tutilli had told her must be decisive, came on.

Despite his weakness, the next day William wanted to ride again in the fresh air. The physician, Dr. Cartelach, whispered to Elizabeth that he might die in the attempt. Since there was no possibility of a refusal, it was concluded that opposition to William's request was worse than the risk. William was carried down in a chair and supported in Elizabeth's trembling arms with pillows as they began their ride through Pisa to view the Leaning Tower, but in five minutes they were forced to return home. To get William out of the coach and in the chair, up the stairs, and on the bed "words never can tell," wrote Elizabeth. With a day's rest in between, William's complaint seemed lessened and he again wanted to ride. Madame De Tot, the lady of the house, accompanied the Setons. When William returned home, he seemed in better spirits and more able to help himself. Elizabeth really began to think that riding was good for him, but that was the last ride. From then on, he was in constant suffering.

It was now Christmas Eve, and William was confined to his bed. The violent disorder of his bowels made him think that he could not last until morning. Elizabeth wrote Rebecca that William talked with cheerfulness about his "darlings," and thanked God with great earnestness that He had given him so much time to reflect on His word with its accompanying consolations. Through the use of a small portion of laudanum, William rested until midnight. When he awoke, he noticed that Elizabeth had not lain down. She answered him, "No, love, for the sweetest reflections kept me awake. Christmas day is begun. The day of our dear Redeemer's birth is the day that opened to us the door of everlasting life."[27] When William expressed his desire to have the Sacrament, Elizabeth felt she must do all she could. She put a little wine in a glass and said different parts of Psalms and prayers which she had marked in her prayer book. They took "the cup of thanksgiving and set aside the sorrows of time in the views of eternity, happy to find its joys strongly painted to him." William asked Elizabeth then, as he had often done, if she felt certain that his failings were forgiven and that he would be admitted to heaven. In answer, she always tried to convince him that when a soul such as his had been so sincere and so submissive to God's will, it would be sinful to doubt one moment that he would be saved through the merits of Jesus, our Redeemer.

When Captain O'Brien and Mr. Filicchi came to visit William that day, William, with a composure and solemnity that made them all cold, gave Elizabeth into Captain O'Brien's charge to take home and thanked God that now he was not wanted for the support of his family. Because of his extreme weakness, he had a strange fancy in his mind that he had received a letter from the Lottery Office in London telling him that Elizabeth's ticket which he had renewed there had drawn the royal prize. His brother, James, had also written that he owed not a single bill in the world. In this, Elizabeth did not contradict James since it was a source of great comfort to William. Captain O'Brien and Mr. Filicchi agreed that they must let him think so.

In great pain, William was so impatient to be gone on Christmas that he continually called his Redeemer to pardon and release him. Elizabeth spent the day on her knees at William's bedside every moment that she could. Prayer seemed to be his only relief. When she stopped to give him anything, she could hardly persuade him to wet his lips.

> Why do you do it? What do I want? I want to be in heaven. Pray, pray for my soul! This day my Redeemer took pain and sorrow that I might have peace. This day he gained eternal life for me.[28]

Elizabeth prayed earnestly for him that his pardon might be sealed in heaven and then laid her head on the chair by which she knelt and lost herself in sleep. She wrote of the incident to Rebecca:

> I saw in my slumber a little angel with a pen in one hand, and a sheet of pure white paper in the other. He looked at me, holding out the paper, and wrote in large letters, "Jesus."[29]

When Elizabeth awoke and told her vision to William, it was a great comfort to him. Very much affected by it, he repeated, "The angel wrote 'Jesus.' He has opened the door of eternal life for me, and will cover me with his mantle."[30]

At midnight when the cold sweat came on, he would reach out both his arms and say repeatedly, "You promised me you would go; come, come, fly." At four, the hard struggle ceased and he began to sob. Scarcely audible, he repeated, "My dear wife and little ones"; "My Christ Jesus, have mercy and receive me," was all Elizabeth could distinguish. When she asked him if he felt he was going to his Redeemer, he answered, "Yes," with a look of peace. As he always wanted his door shut, Elizabeth had no interruptions. At a quarter past seven on Tuesday morning,

December 27, 1803, while Elizabeth was still praying and holding his hand, William died without a groan or struggle. Elizabeth, too, was released from a "struggle next to death." As she knelt at his deathbed, she expressed her gratitude to God for relieving William of his suffering and experienced joy at the assurance that he was now with God.

Elizabeth then opened the door to let the servants and the landlady know that William had died. As fearful of catching his illness as the people in New York were of yellow fever, they were at a loss at what to do. Elizabeth then asked two women who had previously washed for William to assist her in preparing his body for burial, and again shut the door. She wrote Rebecca that with their help, she did the last duties, laid him out herself, and felt she had done all, "All that tenderest love and duty could do."[31] William had told Elizabeth to tell her friends not to weep for him, that he died happy and satisfied with the Almighty will.

During William's last agony, Elizabeth had not rested for a week; the last three days and three nights the fatigue had been incessant, and she had only one meal in twenty-four hours. Still she had to wash, dress, pack up and in one hour be in Mrs. Filicchi's carriage ready to ride fifteen miles to Leghorn to arrange for William's burial. Guy Carleton and Louis, the faithful servant in the Lazaretto, kept watch. William's body was brought to Leghorn in the afternoon and deposited in the "burying house" (a chapel) in the Protestant cemetery to await burial the next morning. Exhausted, Elizabeth wrote Rebecca that night,

> Oh! What a day! Close his eyes, lay him out, ride a journey, be obliged to see a dozen people in my room till night, and at night crowded with the whole sense of my situation. O, my Father and my God! [was all she could exclaim].[32]

By eleven o'clock the next day, the English and Americans in Leghorn attended the funeral services for William Seton. The Reverend Mr. Thomas Hall, the Protestant Chaplain at the British consulate, presided at the burial. When it was over, Elizabeth felt gratified that she had shown every respect for William's wishes as he had expressed them to her. In her account to Rebecca, she wrote:

> In all this, it is not necessary to dwell on the mercy and consoling presence of my dear Lord, for no mortal strength could support what I experienced.[33]

William's suffering and death had interested so many persons in Leghorn that Elizabeth felt she was as kindly treated and as much attended to, as if she were home. She and William had met with nothing but kindness even in servants and strangers. The Filicchi wives, Amabilia and Mary Cowper, showed Elizabeth the most tender sympathy, compassion and understanding. Amabilia welcomed her into her home until arrangements could be made for her return to New York. Writing to Rebecca, she noted, "It seems, indeed, they cannot do enough." Among the persons who visited her that first night, besides the Filicchis and the Rev. Mr. Hall, Elizabeth made special mention of the Commandant, "who came," she wrote Rebecca, "with a black band around his arm and his hat, and was so compassionate toward poor Signora. All his kindness at the Lazaretto was in evidence now." Indeed, when she looked forward to her unprovided earthly situation, she was the more touched by their tenderness.

In the care of the kind Filicchis with whom she remained until her departure for New York, Elizabeth took every opportunity to visit William's grave. Each time she went, she wept over it with "inexpressible tenderness and unrestrained affection" as she reflected on his last sufferings and recalled their happy times together. She wrote Rebecca, "It seemed that I loved him more than anyone could love on earth."

CHAPTER 5

Antonio Filicchi
My Friend Becomes My Brother

Shortly after the death of Elizabeth Seton's husband, arrangements were made for her return to New York on the *Shepherdess*. In the interim, Amabilia and Mary (Cowper), the wives of Antonio and Filippo, wished to acquaint Elizabeth with their culture. To this end, they planned a tour of the palaces, museums and churches in Florence and the environs of Leghorn. Above all, they thought, Elizabeth would become better versed in knowledge of the Catholic faith and its practices. They had previously taken the initiative to introduce her to their best informed priest, Abbé Peter Plunkett, an Irishman, and had found her very willing to listen to his and their enlightening conversations. Elizabeth's main interest was keeping friends with all of them.

By January 4, 1804, Elizabeth, her daughter, Anna Maria (then called Annina) and Amabilia were lodged in the Palace of the Medici which fronts the Arno River and presents an elegant view of the mountains — *Monti Morelli*. Among the first sites they visited were the Pitti Palace, the residence of Queen Maria Louise with its innumerable suites, the adjacent Boboli Gardens, the Uffizi Gallery (Academy of Sculpture), and the Botanical Gardens. In each case, Elizabeth was overwhelmed with their richness and artistic beauty. The Uffizi Gallery, she felt, was beyond description. Overcome with the beauty of the plants and flowers in the Botanical Gardens, she tried to imagine the beauty of the Garden of Paradise.

More than anything else, Elizabeth was overjoyed when on Sunday they visited the Church of the Annunziata. On entering the church, she was impressed by what she saw before her: hundreds of people, young and old, men and women, kneeling everywhere about the altar praying, as inattentive to visitors as if they were not there. The soft music lifted her heart to a foretaste of heavenly pleasures. While Amabilia went on errands, Elizabeth and Annina had the pleasure of visiting the Church of San Firenze with two of the nuns from the adjacent convent. Elizabeth was so touched by the scene of the young priest unlocking the little chapel that her heart willingly followed him into the church.

The next day saw the tourists in the Church of San Lorenzo. As Elizabeth approached the marble, jewel-studded main altar, she was struck so forcibly by its beauty that the *Magnificat* came to her mind and absorbed every other feeling. It reminded her of the Old Testament biblical story and the adornments of the Temple of Jerusalem. Later, in the Church of Santa Maria Novella, Elizabeth stood beneath the life-size picture of the *Descent from the Cross*. Pondering how Mary's eyes were fixed on Jesus, and how she must have felt, Elizabeth found it hard to leave that picture. Often, thereafter, she would shut her eyes and try to recall the painting to her imagination.

When she turned to the painting of Abraham and Isaac, she felt the whole convulsion of the Patriarch's breast as he readied himself to sacrifice his son. She could hide the tears, but the shaking of her whole body could not be so easily hidden.

While Elizabeth and her companions were in Florence, Antonio Filicchi, Amabilia's husband, wrote Elizabeth a very warm and touching letter:

> Your dear William was the early friend of my youth; you are now come in his room. Your soul is even dearer to Antonio and will be so forever. May the good Almighty God enlighten your mind and strengthen your heart to see and follow in Religion the surest true way to eternal blessings. I shall call for you in Paradise, if it is decreed that the vast plains of the Ocean shall be betwixt us. Don't discontinue meanwhile to pray, to knock at the door. I am confident that our Redeemer will not be deaf to the humble prayers of so dear a creature.[1]

In return, Elizabeth, who looked upon friednship as a blessing from God and who regarded Antonio as one dear to her William and already dear to herself, answered:

> We often receive blessings from the hand of God and convert them into evils. This has hitherto been my fault in respect to a very sincere and uncommon affection I have for you and I am determined with God's help no more to abuse the very great favor He bestows on me in giving me your friendship and in the future will endeavor to show you how much I value it by doing all I can to contribute to your happiness — on your part I intreat [sic] you will behave to me with confidence and affection — the more you confide in me, the more careful I shall be — trust me and the angel.[2]

Out of admiration for her "so delicate, so easy, so witty a style," Antonio quickly replied:

> Believe me, my beloved sister, that for the purpose of obtaining one of your letters in a week, I could cheerfully . . . [scribble] all the 24 hours of the day.[3]

About the middle of January, Elizabeth, Annina and Amabilia left Florence to return to Leghorn and await the departure of the *Shepherdess*, presumably to set sail around the end of the month. Upon their return, Antonio Filicchi welcomed the travellers home. "With a look of many sympathies," he helped Elizabeth from the carriage and showed her to her room. Here Mrs. Filicchi and "sweet Ann" gazed in her face to comfort her, as Elizabeth felt the anguish of not being with her little ones and Rebecca in New York.

Antonio later informed Elizabeth and Annina that the *Shepherdess* would not be ready to leave Leghorn until February 18. Accustomed as she was to disappointments, Elizabeth made the best of events. The delay was quite providential, the Filicchis thought, since it afforded Elizabeth and the Filicchi family the opportunity to strengthen their bond of friendship. On the day scheduled to leave, Elizabeth and Annina were safe on board the *Shepherdess* which was ready to hoist sails the next morning. But on the next morning, they were brought the news that a driving storm had come up during the night and had struck their vessel against another ship anchored in port. While the ship was being examined, the Setons were obliged to return to shore.

When they boarded the ship a second time, Elizabeth suffered more disappointment. Annina, unable to hide her suffering, had a high fever and was covered with an eruption which Dr. Tutilli, the Filicchis' physician, diagnosed as scarlet fever. Elizabeth was willing to risk the life of the child and go back to America, but when Captain O'Brien told her that if he kept them on board, he could not get a bill of health for Barcelona and that the quarantine would ruin his voyage, Elizabeth was forced to stay in Leghorn. The Filicchis welcomed their guests most kindly, but Elizabeth's heart was "down enough" at the disappointment. It was not long until Elizabeth herself was taken ill and like Anna spent twenty days confined to her room.

As the days and weeks passed by, Elizabeth had time to reflect and pray. She became more and more familiar with the daily practices and beliefs of the Catholic faith. Deeply taken with the doctrine that Catholics possess God in the Blessed Sacrament, she felt the full sadness of her tears each time the priest passed her window carrying the Blessed Sacrament to the sick and dying. In the very house of the Filicchis there was a chapel with the Blessed Sacrament. People in this country could also go to Mass every morning, if they wished, as early as four o'clock, so different from the practice in her own Trinity Church in New York. She recalled how she and her sister-soul, Rebecca Seton, would say as the church door was closing on them: "No more until next Sunday." By the time Elizabeth was ready to leave Leghorn, she was completely fascinated by the Catholic faith. If she did not believe, it would not be for want of praying.

Before Elizabeth and Annina were to leave Leghorn, the Filicchis took them to the shrine of *La Madonna delle Grazie* in Montenero, a beautiful part of the country not far from Leghorn. In the shrine chapel of Our Lady at Mass that day, at the very moment of the consecration, a young Englishman said aloud in her ear: "This is what they call their Real Presence." When she heard this comment, Elizabeth, deeply distressed, bent to the floor. Her eyes filled with tears as she recalled the words of Saint Paul: "They discern not the Lord's body."[4] This experience provoked the greatest moment of faith in her life.

One evening as she stood by the window with the moon shining full on Antonio Filicchi's face, he raised his eyes to heaven and showed her how to make the sign of the cross. As she made it, the thought of the sign of the cross on her body left her cold. But she recalled the story in the Book of Revelation and reflected on how the letter "T" with which the angel was to sign the forehead of those who were saved was a cross.

Several weeks later, Antonio Filicchi brought Elizabeth the news that the *Pyomingo*, New York bound, was anchored in the Leghorn harbor. When Elizabeth learned that preparations were being made to book passage on that ship, she could not contain her joy. But since a Captain John Blagge, a very young man and unknown to the Filicchis, was to take the Setons back to America, they had many fears for the young widow and her daughter travelling alone under those conditions, besides the danger of pirates and hostile cruisers which was always present. Even if the Setons were given letters of recommendation, these would not afford sufficient protection.

Thus, the Filicchi brothers Antonio and Filippo, together with Antonio's wife, Amabilia, decided that Antonio should accompany Elizabeth and Annina on the return trip to New York to guarantee their safety and at the same time to look into the Filicchi business affairs in America and Canada. The morning of April 8, 1804, finally arrived when Elizabeth was to bid farewell to her dear friends in Leghorn.

While the stars were yet bright, Elizabeth went to Mass with Antonio and Amabilia. In the Church of Santa Catarina, they would ask a blessing on the voyage, pray for the souls of her dear William and of her father, and for all her dear ones awaiting her return. At Mass, Elizabeth, observing Amabilia and Antonio going to Holy Communion, felt keenly that she could not receive her Redeemer. Compared to the faith of the Filicchis, Elizabeth felt that she had but "dear ashes." But, she asked herself, did she not beg God to give her their faith and promise Him all in return for such a gift? As she and Annina looked on Antonio's and Amabilia's tender parting, they experienced strange tears of joy mixed with grief. Elizabeth's heart was sorrowful at parting from friends who had been so kind to her, especially as she thought of the Filicchi children whom she tenderly loved. At the same time she experienced the joy of once more embarking for home.

Down at the harbor, while Elizabeth, Annina and Antonio waited for the *Pyomingo's* last signal to call them on board, Filippo's last blessing to Elizabeth was that of the truest friend. "Oh, Filicchi," she said to him, "do not witness against me! May God bless you forever and may you shine as the 'stars in glory' for what you have done for me!" Filippo threw out his last challenge to her: "I meet you on the Day of Judgment." As the sun rose full on the wharf where they stood, Antonio passed through the struggles of parting from his family. "Dear manly soul," wrote Elizabeth, "who, indeed, appears to me as the image of God."[5]

At eight o'clock, Elizabeth, Annina and Antonio were sitting quietly on deck. The anchor had been raised and the sails hoisted. During this voyage of fifty-six days, the seafarers would pray, fast and celebrate the special feast days of the Church as much as they could. Then, too, Antonio would instruct Elizabeth in the tenets of the Catholic faith. Under his direction, she would read Alban Butler's *Lives of the Saints*, and keep her Bible continuously at hand.

As the days passed, Elizabeth began to experience strong desires to manifest her love and gratitude to Antonio whom she had first seen as the "image of God." From the hour when she thought her "foot was going to slip" she called on God's mercy to sustain her in these temptations. Her prayer was not only for herself but also for Antonio. "If the enemy from whom we cannot escape should appear before us, we will look him in the face, invoking thy name, Jesus, Jesus, Jesus," she noted in her *Journal*.[6]

With God's grace, Elizabeth was able to resist the growing number of her passionate temptations. If she had yielded to them, they would have lessened not only her own self-esteem, but also the love both she and Antonio professed for God, and the deep affection the two friends had for each other. She penned this striking passage:

> When a soul puts all its trust in God, feeling itself prepared to renounce everything and to consider the dearest ties of life as less than nothing when compared to the worth of his love; when this soul having seriously resolved to serve and obey God, sees itself attacked by the lower instincts of nature, and in spite of its prayers, tears, penances, the more rigorous, tempted at least apparently to yield to the humiliating suggestions of evil, oh, this is assuredly the work of the enemy of salvation.... But how is that? Doesn't he know that we have sworn inviolable fidelity to our Lord?[7]

As they continued their journey homeward sailing on the blue waters of the Mediterranean and skirting the coast of Spain, they passed through the Strait of Gibraltar to the Atlantic Ocean. Elizabeth reminisced about her William's bitter sufferings, and looked forward to seeing her children again and the loved ones whom she had left in New York. On June 3, 1804, with grateful joy, Elizabeth sighted land

and the port of New York, all the while remembering all that Antonio had done for her.

Back in New York away from her Catholic friends and influences, Elizabeth looked to Antonio Filicchi for encouragement. Her letters to him during this period reveal the depth of their friendship and Elizabeth's "uncommon affection" and love for Antonio, her "best brother and true friend of her soul." When her Protestant friends learned of her growing desire to become a Catholic, they abandoned her to her doubts and scruples. Antonio, too, weary of her hesitancies, left New York for Boston on business. Alone with her reluctancies, Elizabeth placed her confidence in God and trusted that by her prayers, God would manifest His will to her and lead her to the true Church of Christ. Once Elizabeth's mind was settled on the truth of the Catholic faith, then she wrote Antonio about the burnings of her soul.

To prove as much as possible her affection for Antonio and to give him pleasure, Elizabeth delighted in writing him letters. Over and over, she avowed to him her affection and love in gratitude for his interest in her soul and for his benefactions during her sojourn in Leghorn. One morning while he was still in New York, she lost him in the crowd. Looking for him, she wondered why he had not looked for her, if only as an exercise of his usual charity. He should know how much she would be disappointed at returning home without his fraternal benediction. "Do love your poor sister," she wrote him, "if not for her sake and for the love she bears you, yet for *His sake* whose law is love."[8]

While Antonio was on his business trips to Boston, Philadelphia and Montreal, Elizabeth longed to hear from him. Wistfully every evening, she began to watch for James Seton's carriage, hoping that he would bring a letter from Antonio. Day after day passed without a line. But Elizabeth trusted in God that he was safe and had only deferred writing because of multiplied engagements and the pleasure of new acquaintances. She hoped, too, that he was not suffering from the winter. When he wished to add a "cordial drop of sweetness to her cup," he should write her some thoughts of his soul. If he was too lazy to write, she would appreciate his blessings. When only a few lines rewarded her anxious anticipation, she was disappointed.

Pained at his seeming neglect, Elizabeth wondered if it was possible that he would excuse himself to her on the score of diffidence and ignorance of the English language. During the weeks that had passed in which she had not heard from him, far from feeling less interest for him or less value for his affection, she prayed for him more earnestly and anxiously. She wanted never to think of him with tenderness, except when calling on Almighty God to bless him. Then, often indeed, her heart overflowed, and the tears of affection which at other times she had carefully repressed poured out.

Elizabeth tried to be indifferent to Antonio's neglect. The moments she spent writing to or thinking of him were given to Jesus, who never disappointed her but who repaid every instant with hours of peace and unfailing contentment. She wrote Antonio that the tenderest interest he could ever bestow on her was only a stream of which Jesus is the fountain. If his charity has passed from New York to Boston, she would be satisfied with everything, if he were only well. While she was writing to him, the winter storms in New York had already begun and blew her candle out.

Several weeks had passed when a letter arrived from Antonio, "like a cordial to her heart." Elizabeth was so joyful that she set the piano wide open and let the children dance until they were tired. They had crowded around her as they always did when a letter came from Antonio with the repeated question: "When will he come, mamma?" She was obliged to pretend that he had sent a message of love to each of them. Her first emotion in reading the letter was one of thankfulness for the "many proofs" he had given of his interest and pity for his "poor little sister." In the sure confidence of his mind, she felt he must smile at her expressions as "the effusions of a heated imagination," but her soul and the souls of her children were at stake.

Elizabeth found Antonio's stay in Boston long and was anxious for his return to New York. She counted the months: October, November, December and January had already passed. For some weeks she had been watching and waiting for the footsteps of the only one she could now welcome with her heart within her doors. For her Protestant relatives had isolated her. This must have sounded shocking to him, she thought, but he knew the contradictions of her heart concerning the depth of the Catholic faith and should not wonder if she had wished to "dwell in a cave or desert." "But no more of this," she wrote him. Her thoughts must return to the lesson of "God's will be done."[9]

Until Antonio mentioned that a lawsuit was detaining him in Boston, she could not help imagining that "some extravagance" such as that which once bound him to his "American sister" had influenced his stay. Consequently, he was the constant companion of her thoughts and prayers. In his next letter, Antonio wrote Elizabeth that he was feeling the benefit of her prayers and believed he was never better in his life than now.

In Antonio's absence, Elizabeth became increasingly unsettled in the Catholic faith. The Reverend Henry Hobart, the Episcopalian minister at Trinity Church, heard of her plight and sent her an affectionate note asking her how she could ever think of leaving the church in which she was baptized. What he was not aware of was the concern of

Elizabeth's many friends that brought them to visit her every day at her home. Nor did he know of their invitations to join their particular churches. Among them, Mary, the Methodist, Elizabeth's good servant, "groaned and contemplated" that Elizabeth's soul was so misled because she had yet no convictions.

Elizabeth felt, however, that even if she had never met the Filicchis, the books which the Rev. Mr. Hobart had given her to read would have suggested a thousand uncertainties to her about the Protestant faith. Nowhere did she find in them the claim or even the admission of the apostolic loosening of sins. Besides, she was disturbed to read in Isaac Newton's *Prophecies* that only "a few are saved." In brief, the sum total of its teachings revolted her heart for she knew they were "all black accusations against the Catholics."

When she passed the Catholic church, she stopped and read the tombstones, lifting up her heart to God for pity and appealing to Him as her judge. How joyfully she would enter there and kiss the steps of His altar, visit Him every day and pour out her soul before Him, but she dared not bring there a doubtful, disturbed mind, a confusion of fears and hesitations, lest it would offend Him whom alone she desired to please. Often, indeed, almost continually, her thoughts wandered to Leghorn. She recalled her room under Antonio's roof, the appearance of every object from the window and the smile of "darling Patrizio" on his tiptoes asking questions of her. She remembered the little chapel in the Church of Santa Catarina where she could see the priest, his every feature and action before her. She could hear the bell and see the "cup" elevated and feel her spirit lying "in the dust before God." At times, she felt obliged to make the sign of the cross and look up to God for pity.

On the feast day of the Nativity of the Blessed Virgin Mary, Elizabeth tried to sanctify the day by begging God to look into her soul and see how gladly she would kiss Mary's feet because she was His Mother. Joyfully, she would show every expression of reverence more than even Antonio would desire, if she could do it with that "freedom of soul which glowed from the knowledge of God's will." In Leghorn, she had prayed the *Memorare*, Saint Bernard's prayer to Our Lady, and felt that she had found her own mother in Mary.

The Scriptures, once her delight and comfort, became a continual source of pain; every page she opened confounded her. Twelve months before when the six weekdays were past, she joyfully looked to Sunday as a full reward for whatever sorrow or care she had passed through in the week. Now she looked fearfully at the setting sun, dreading that a fine morning should find her with no excuse for avoiding church.

At times, the sense of her real situation pressed so strong on her mind that it almost overpowered her. The horror of neglecting to hear God's voice (if He had, indeed, spoken to her through Antonio), or of resisting Him (if, indeed, the warnings and declarations of her old friends were truth), was shocking to her. Asking for Antonio's pity, she wrote him:

> If your church is antichrist, your worship idolatrous, my soul shares the crime, though my will would resist it, for O, my Brother, if you could know the shocking and awful objects presented to my mind in opposition to your church, you would say it is impossible, except a voice from heaven directed, that I ever could become a member of it.[10]

Her sins, recalled before God, struck Elizabeth with a total darkness so that she wondered how she could expect from

Him the light of His truth. She prayed that her broken and contrite heart might find mercy through the sufferings of Christ.

Elizabeth could not make any decision without looking again at the Catholic position and asking some questions for her relief and comfort. Over and over she had read the promises of Our Lord given to St. Peter on the loosening of sins and read every day the sixth chapter of John's Gospel on Jesus, the Bread of Life. Then questioning herself, she asked: "Can I offend him [God] by believing those express words?"[11] She had also reread St. Francis de Sales' *Introduction to the Devout Life* which Filippo Filicchi had given her while in Leghorn and asked herself: "Is it possible that I shall think differently from him or seek heaven any other way?"[12] When she read Alban Butler's *Lives of the Saints* which Antonio had recommended to her, they seemed to lessen her troubles and made them as nothing. In reading the *Following of Christ* [the *Imitation of Christ*] by Thomas à Kempis, a Catholic writer, she noted that its Protestant preface said he was well versed in the knowledge of Scripture. Reflecting on him and again on St. Francis de Sales, she exclaimed: "Will I ever know how to please God better than they did?"

In all this, Elizabeth felt assured that God would not despise her prayer which was fixed on His word. She begged God to direct her, for it was in vain to look for help from any but Him. When she passed over the street that led to the Catholic church, with struggling heart she prayed: "O, teach me, teach me, where to go?" Antonio's letter assured her that through the name of "Jesus," her prayer would be answered. She looked again to the *Jesus Psalter*, a little book that Antonio had given her, and made it her companion.

Elizabeth's prayer was soon to be answered. On the feast of the Epiphany, January 6, 1805, for the pure

ANTONIO FILICCHI... MY FRIEND BECOMES MY BROTHER

enjoyment of reading a good homily, Elizabeth took up a volume of the French Jesuit, the Rev. Louis Bourdaloue, and opened it to the homily of that day. When she read those words: "O you who have lost the star of faith!" anguish and distress rushed upon her. Bourdaloue had made the point that when we no longer can discern the "star of faith," we must look for it where alone it can be found — with the depositors of His word. Elizabeth's immediate desire was to see a Catholic priest. She made an effort to see the Rev. Matthew O'Brien at Saint Peter's Church on Barclay Street in New York City, but was disappointed at not finding him there. Pinning her faith on God alone, she would wait for Antonio's return from Boston and take her children with her to the Catholic church.

Without knowing that it was Ash Wednesday, on February 27, 1805, Elizabeth entered Saint Peter's Catholic Church. Her heart seemed to die away in silence before the Tabernacle. "O, my God, here let me rest!" she prayed. The Rev. O'Brien, an Irish priest who had just arrived at Saint Peter's, talked of death so familiarly that he delighted and revived her. She was reminded of the "worthy clergymen" in Boston whom Antonio had written her about. If only she could hear the sermons of the learned and eloquent Rev. John Cheverus.

Upon his return to New York in early March, Antonio suggested that she write to Fr. Cheverus for instruction, comfort and advice. A few days later in his reply, Fr. Cheverus told Elizabeth that she had heard enough argument on both sides and that she was "never for a moment a strong Protestant," but was, he believed, "always a good Catholic." The doubts which had arisen in her mind did not destroy her faith, but only disturbed her mind, he informed her. Thus her decision to become a Catholic she found strengthened by his advice to join the Catholic Church as soon as possible and, when doubts arose, to say only: "I believe, O Lord, help Thou my (un)belief."

Elizabeth entered the Church immediately afterward on March 14, 1805. Her formal abjuration took place at Saint Peter's Church. Antonio Filicchi was her sponsor. Without delay, Elizabeth began to prepare herself for Confession and Holy Communion. To insure a good absolution, she would readily confess her sins on the housetop. In Fr. O'Brien's role in the sacrament, she saw Christ alone. She counted the days and hours until her First Communion.

The evening before the special day when she was to receive God, she wrote in her *Journal*:

> My God! to the last breath of life, will I not remember this night of watching for morning's dawn, the fearful beating heart so pressing to be gone, the long walk to town, but every step counted nearer that street then nearer that Tabernacle, the nearer the moment He would enter the poor, poor little dwelling so all His own.[13]

The next day on the feast of Our Lady's Annunciation, March 25, Elizabeth made her First Communion. "At last, God is mine and I am His!" she exclaimed. With Jesus in her heart, Elizabeth felt that she had received the most perfect happiness she could enjoy on earth. She hoped that Antonio, too, would fully share in her happiness. If she had had a world to pay him with, it would have been all his for the part he had played in leading her to the true Shepherd of her soul. But, she recollected, there is another scene where he, the "friend, protector, consoler of the widow and fatherless" would be rewarded as her heart desired.

Elizabeth's fancy for Antonio's and her happiness carried her to the Garden of Paradise where he promised to call for her. There, without barrier to their affection, she might enjoy the blessing of being one of his inseparable companions forever. Moreover, it delighted her to consider that even here and now her affection for Antonio (though he had drawn the line) could not be hidden from the God Who sees her heart in its sincerity, simplicity and holiness. With her whole heart, she had committed Antonio to God or she should have been very unhappy. The peace that came over her in Holy Communion supplied her with strength and resolution beyond anything she could have conceived possible in her frail body.

One day after Antonio had returned to Boston, she wrote him her experiences to show the steadfastness of her soul. That day, she had passed through fire in the number of people she had accidentally encountered. Every one smiled, some with affection, some with civility. In the midst of all the conversations of the "good ladies" and her brother-in-law, Dr. Wright Post, about her conversion, the Lord greatly cleared her way. Whenever she was questioned as to the state of her soul, she told them instantly and decidedly that the time for reasoning and opinion was past. Nor could she be ungrateful to God after the powerful convictions He had so graciously given her. To speak one moment on the subject would certainly have offended Him. Her heart free of all concern, she redoubled her prayers and prepared herself for the next day's Communion. She was happy to tell Antonio that she had taken part of a very neat house about half way to town near Greenwich Street where she would be able to go every morning to church before breakfast and there visit her Master. Her good friend, Catherine Dupleix, had mentioned that she always told the kind ladies who every day shed tears for "the poor deluded Mrs. Seton" how happy she was that anything in this world could comfort and console Elizabeth.

In her letters, Elizabeth was not unmindful of Antonio's children and his "sweet Amabilia." In one letter, particularly, his account of the children delighted her. The idea of Georgino's loveliness pleased her as much as if she had been his parent. If she could ever hold him to her heart again, she would experience sweet pleasure. Her own boys were "mad with joy" at going to Saint Peter's Church where they could see the cross. William, her eldest son, always begged to be a "little priest" (altar boy). He declared that he would rather be one than the "richest greatest man in the world." Indeed, Elizabeth received much pleasure in seeing her children make the sign of the cross, and kneel devoutly in the presence of Jesus.

As Antonio prepared to return to Leghorn, Elizabeth thanked God with every power in her soul for the favorable prospects in his business. She had heard how much he had been engaged in his work and, at times, vexed when some affairs were troublesome to him. Besides, he had had many letters to prepare for Leghorn. Strangers, too, were pressing him with invitations. Then, not the least of his duties was Confession and Communion which also required his attention. She would be most happy if upon his return to Leghorn he could say his business ventures in America and Canada were successful.

When the time came for Antonio to leave New York, Elizabeth asked God to bless him and the "angel of his presence" to accompany him on his journey to Leghorn. This would restore him at last to Amabilia, "the happy heart who claimed him as her own."

Through the years, Elizabeth's affection for Antonio and her gratitude to him for putting her steps on the right path to eternal happiness never diminished. To the very last, she asked him to love her and bless her and to remember her always in his prayers. In one of her last letters to him she wrote: "I long to hear that you are well. The love of my heart can never grow cold to you and your dear family while it has a beat of life."[14]

Elizabeth Seton's one earthly desire was to spend eternity in heaven with her friends. Rebecca Seton, her sister-soul, the subject of the next chapter, was no exception.

CHAPTER 6

Rebecca Seton:
My Sister-In-Law And Dearest Friend

Elizabeth Seton had by 1798 charmed and won the respect of the Seton family and soon had become her widowed father-in-law's (William Seton, Sr.) confidant in the many details of his career. He had shown her treasured letters that no one else was to see. At his death in June 1798, Elizabeth suddenly found herself the head of his large family of thirteen children.

Of Mr. Seton's seven youngest children, the offspring of his second marriage, only Rebecca, then eighteen, was old enough to accept responsibility and to be of some help to Elizabeth. Writing to her friend Julia Scott about the situation, she told her that the children were attractive, and that she loved them as her own. Then she added:

> Rebecca is, without any exception, the most truly amiable, estimable young woman I ever knew. Her virtues are such as would ornament any station, and does honor to my poor father [William Seton, her father-in-law] who was her only director in everything.[1]

To Rebecca, then, Elizabeth opened her heart and shared her most intmate feelings and experiences, as to a sister-soul and dear friend.

Once when Elizabeth was in Staten Island, she could not refrain from telling Rebecca in New York that even though they were miles apart there could be no distance between their souls. Elizabeth seldom swept the hall or dressed the flower pots, or walked around the pear-tree walk without feeling accompanied by Rebecca as though she were actually at her side. While Elizabeth was surrounded by many persons dear to her heart, she seemed to want Rebecca always near her. "Her society is a source of pleasure to me, such as is altogether new and unexpected," she wrote Julia.[2]

Until Elizabeth had been living under the same roof with Rebecca, she had always thought her an uninformed girl of many neglected qualities. But every day proved to Elizabeth the contrary as she became more and more dependent on Rebecca's company. One morning, with Kit (Catherine Josephine) in her arms, the moment Elizabeth saw the bright sunshine, she was thinking of the absent Rebecca and sharply wanting her presence. Once, when Rebecca was away attending one of her sisters during pregnancy, Elizabeth wrote her father, Dr. Bayley: With Rebecca away their "little circle had lost its key." Frequently the women of the house would look out towards Rebecca's house and see distinctly the street door shut and the dining room windows opened where normally Rebecca could be observed.

What Rebecca could not know was what melancholy thoughts her absence caused Elizabeth. Ever since the latter had heard that Rebecca was to spend the winter with her brother, Jack, in Delaware, Elizabeth feared that Rebecca would soon forget the times they had spent together. Elizabeth, knowing full well Jack's decidedly adverse opinion of her, was sure of one thing: if Rebecca once got under his roof, she would never again be allowed to call Elizabeth's home her own.

Upon Rebecca's return from her brother Jack's house, she was asked not to forget Elizabeth's request that she be as much as possible with her "lonely sister." Elizabeth claimed to have ten thousand things to say to her "sweet Beck." Rather than write them, she had thought it best to wait until they got snug at their work on the sofa. For Rebecca to give Elizabeth one week out of six could not be doing wrong to anyone, Elizabeth thought, especially since she might be recruiting members for the society of the Ladies of Charity. They could then sit together on the outdoor balcony viewing the bay, or at the inside piano, singing their hearts out. Elizabeth asked Rebecca to write the very moment she saw the way clear for a visit, and to name the day she could be expected.

Elizabeth seldom missed an opportunity to invite Rebecca to join her little family. For example, on one occasion, William was to take Anna Maria, Cecilia (Rebecca's youngest sister) and their two sons, Will and Richard, for breakfast at their Aunt Farquhar's, then to Saint Mark's Church for services, and from there to Mrs. Kemble's for dinner. So, Elizabeth wrote Rebecca to tell her that she must come, if possible, to be with them. Elizabeth was eager to see Rebecca's smiles, and felt that Rebecca, too, would enjoy seeing theirs.

Yet Elizabeth was not totally possessive of Rebecca. Elizabeth even reminded Rebecca that she had a duty to reach out to others. Elizabeth knew of the preference of Mary Seton Wilkes (a distant relative of William and Rebecca Seton) for Rebecca and of the influence which Rebecca, more than anyone else, exerted over Mary. She wanted Rebecca to try to teach Mary, for the sake of her own happiness, to look at the events of life as guided by a just and merciful God Who through trials and disappointments, strives to turn the soul to Himself. In the case of their friend Lidy, Elizabeth was sure that if anyone could teach Lidy how to draw closer to God, it would be Rebecca. She hoped Lidy would accompany Rebecca to Sunday services and that they would all meet there.

One Sunday when Elizabeth could not attend the service, she looked across Staten Island from her father's Health Establishment to Saint Paul's steeple in New York, her thoughts reverting to Rebecca and the Rev. Henry Hobart, their minister. She sent Rebecca a note asking that she give Mr. Hobart a look and a sigh, for her, such as she herself would give and to remember to tell her the text of his homily.

When Elizabeth wrote Rebecca about her children, she tried to recall the things she knew Rebecca would want to hear about each of them. At that very moment, Anna, Will and Dick were down at the Battery. After Will got over his sick spell, he was the merriest of the party and "ran on the beach like a bird." She was persuaded that Dick never saw birds without thinking of "Godma" (Rebecca). He lifted his little hands and made the expression of wonder Rebecca had taught him, then looked all around as if somebody was missing.

As for Kit, everybody in the family knew that she was Rebecca's image. One morning when Elizabeth was out walking with her, Kit held up her little hands with such delight at the beautiful sky that Elizabeth said she "could have eaten her up." Her locks were growing red and she was so saucy that at times managing her was out of the question. If Kit had not been cutting teeth, Elizabeth would have weaned her. When Kit was sick with a burning fever, sore throat and cough, Elizabeth wanted Rebecca not to be uneasy about her godchild. If she were to die then, she would be an angel.

Because of their friendship, Elizabeth revealed the anxieties of her soul to Rebecca, especially those regarding her husband William's poor health. One summer, while William and Rebecca had been in New York and Elizabeth on Staten Island, Elizabeth had asked Rebecca not to let William lose a minute of enjoyment in the sun, for such a "sweet sun and sweet prospect" would soon be shut out from them. The prolonged settlement of their business affairs also kept Elizabeth anxious. Two days before Christmas, 1799, she wrote Rebecca: "Heaven only knows when our troubles will end." Yet hers was a "cheerful sorrow," she said, indescribable except to the sensitive Rebecca. "It is not quite English, but some souls know what it is."[3] At other times Elizabeth believed it best to pass over the unhappy past in silence and not to disturb Rebecca's peace with their present situation.

Elizabeth wrote Rebecca in haste and in pain when expecting her fourth child to arrive in June of that year. She had to make plans for her summer residence and confinement by May. Because it was early spring and nothing had been determined, she felt quite uneasy. If her father could not procure rooms for them on Long Island, she must bear her confinement in their house on Stone Street. This Elizabeth preferred not to do, if it could be avoided. Even when there was nothing pleasant to say, she knew Rebecca would wish a little word from her. Once, she could only tell her that Mammy Huler and Pete were sick, the cook would not stay, and Mrs. Taylor was obese.

But the sharing of sorrows was not one-sided. On one occasion, after a fatiguing morning, Elizabeth received the full impact of an anguished letter which Rebecca had written after her father's death. Elizabeth was hurt a "thousand times more" over the state of Rebecca's mind than over the way the family had imposed on Rebecca's good nature. It seemed to Elizabeth that because Rebecca never complained, the household must have thought that she was stronger than she really was. Elizabeth was gratified, however, when she learned that Rebecca regretted dissembling her true feelings to them.

Uneasy about Rebecca's disposition, Elizabeth sent some of Kit's calcined magnesia and directed her to take it all. She should drink tamarind water or some acid with it. More than anything else, Elizabeth feared that Rebecca's distress of mind would cause the pains in her "breast" to return. Since she could not bear to think that Rebecca was suffering, Elizabeth wanted to hear from her the moment she was better. If she thought Rebecca was in pain while writing, she could receive no pleasure from such letters. She wrote her: "Do nurse yourself, for the most amiable dispositions of the human heart may destroy their possessor if carried too far."[4]

At first when Rebecca had decided to go to her brother Jack's home for a rest, Elizabeth had seemed happy for Rebecca's sake. She was persuaded that the change of air, Jack's affection, and the attention others showered on her would make the change worthwhile. Then, she should return home, with health and peace of mind restored. But, although Elizabeth longed for Rebecca's return home, it pained her to think of it. For the yellow fever epidemic was raging in New York and Rebecca would meet nothing but sorrow. In this plight, Elizabeth's prayer that God's will be done settled her down, and she trusted that it would do the same for Rebecca.

Elizabeth described for Rebecca the scene of the yellow fever victims' suffering. Wherever she looked from the side window of the Health Establishment on Staten Island, she saw lights. Tents were pitched on the grounds of the convalescent house, and a large one adjoined the Dead House. Obsessed by the scene of the dying and the dead, she could not sleep. Babies drained of life by the shipboard fever were perishing on the empty breasts of their expiring mothers. All this while Elizabeth kept telling God that she would gladly give to each of these "poor little creatures" a part of the feeding of her own child, if it depended only on her. She was deeply touched that when the sufferers received their tents and were able to take refuge in them, the first thing they did was to assemble on the grass to pray.

Then death struck within their own circle of friends. Together, Elizabeth and Rebecca assisted at the deathbed of Mary Seton Wilkes. Always alert in the death-watch, they seldom missed the acute suffering of the staring eye, the grasping hand, the distorted limbs and the groaning spirit. When Mary drew her last breath, Elizabeth felt that if the peace overspreading her countenance was an indication of the state of her soul, Mary was now happy. That Mary's heart had been true to God, Elizabeth attributed somewhat to Rebecca's influence.

When Eliza Maitland (Rebecca's half-sister) and her family went to live with Rebecca, Elizabeth knew that Rebecca was heavily burdened with the care and anxiety of the family affairs since she made Eliza's troubles her own. So Elizabeth sent some veal for soup for the ill Eliza along with her letter to Rebecca, and would have sent whatever else Eliza needed, if she had known what to send. To the girls, she sent a letter and a small box of dried sweetmeats. She so much wanted to see Eliza and her "dear chicks" and was impatient to hold the "little one" in her arms, but Elizabeth feared the jaunt to her own house would be too fatiguing for them.

Elizabeth was eager to share with Rebecca any good news. For example, when she heard that James Seton had bought a handsome, three-storey house in Greenwich Street, she thanked God that all of the Setons were not economically sinking. As soon as the Seton-Maitland mercantile business affair was settled, she again wrote Rebecca the good news that the Seton ship, *Liberties*, had docked in New York Harbor and that the victory party involved pouring fifty bowls of tea for three consecutive days causing the sinews of her arms to hurt.

Elizabeth was comforted in her joys and sorrows when peace pervaded Rebecca's soul. On one of these happy occasions, Elizabeth asked Rebecca to kiss "Cele" (Cecilia, Rebecca's sister) for her, and to tell her that she had some beautiful books for her to read when she came home from boarding school. Later, upon her return from the country, Elizabeth sent Rebecca a letter and a package of raisins and almonds to be put in Cecilia's Christmas box. To all in the household (frequently naming each of them), she sent love and affection and prayed that God would bestow His peace on all Rebecca loved best.

When William's health had taken a serious turn for the worse, the Setons had made arrangements to visit the Filicchi family, William's friends in Leghorn, Italy. Down at New York Harbor while they waited for the *Shepherdess* to set sail, Elizabeth had written Rebecca a last-minute note. "I neither look behind, nor before, only up. There is my rest and I want nothing." Then, one night after several weeks on the ocean and after a tiring day, she wrote Rebecca that she had fallen asleep and dreamed that she was in the middle aisle of Trinity Church singing with all her soul the hymn of "our dear sacrament."

Later, while quarantined in the Leghorn Lazaretto, she noted in her *Journal*, meant only for Rebecca, that she had placed all her trust in God. When the "Capitano"-jailer there had asked her if she wanted someone in the cold and barren room with her while she was caring for her husband, she answered him: "Oh, no, what have I to fear?" confident that God would work out everything for their good. Then, remembering God's love and consolations, she wrote in her *Journal*:

> Who can speak of His consolations? What can shut us out from the love of Him Who will dwell with us, through love? How can utterance be given to that which only His spirit can feel?[5]

One day, Elizabeth described to Rebecca how she prayed and read the commentary on the 104th Psalm, sang hymns and laughed, talking to herself of how far God could place her above all sorrow: "With God as our portion, there is no prison in high walls and bolts, no sorrow in the soul that waits on Him."[6] God does not willingly call on His creatures to suffer, Elizabeth thought, but if disappointment did not always appear in the background of the picture, the world would have too much sweetness. While praising God, Elizabeth had accepted William's death as God's will, hoping they would be together again in heaven.

After William was laid to rest, Elizabeth longed to be united with Rebecca and her loved ones in New York. If they did not meet again here, they would surely meet in heaven where there can be no separations. But still Elizabeth longed to tell Rebecca "the sorrows of her heart and the sins of her life." Before leaving Leghorn, she wrote her:

My dear Rebecca, to tell you what God has done for me through my bitter affliction will require many peaceful evenings, which if He has in store for us, we will enjoy with thankful hearts; if not His will be done.[7]

When Elizabeth finally reached New York, she was shocked to discover Rebecca at the point of death. During the month preceding Rebecca's death, together they said the *Te Deum*, the *Miserere* (the 50th Psalm) and part of the Communion service. They talked of death and their heavenly home where they would meet again, never to be separated. The day that Rebecca thought she might die was unusually clear. Pointing to a glowing cloud opposite her window, she said with a cheerful smile: "Dear Sister, if this glimpse of glory is so delightful what must be the presence of God?"[8]

At Rebecca's death, Elizabeth was separated for a time from her "dearest friend"; but, as if to fill the void left in her heart by this friend's death, she learned for the first time what her friendship had meant to Julia Scott.

CHAPTER 7

JULIA SCOTT:
My Worldly Half And Friend In Every Need

Among Elizabeth Seton's early friends, Julia Scott held a very special place in her heart. A friend of Dr. Bayley, she came early into Elizabeth's life. At twenty-four, as a wife and mother, Elizabeth penned these words of reassurance to Julia:

> Difference of age after a certain period is immaterial, and rather adds to affection by creating that kind of confidence we have in those who are at an age to judge of our particular feelings, and yet have more experience to give weight to advice.[1]

Their friendship was destined to last through joy and sorrow, hardship and adversities, health and sickness, family successes and reverses.

The striking contrast between Julia's life-values and Elizabeth's was a matter of utmost concern to Elizabeth. Her many and long letters to Julia Scott reveal her untiring efforts to lift Julia's depressed spirits above her worldly manner of living to thoughts of God. She wrote her: "Be assured Julia, that I love you in my heart, from my heart and with my whole heart."[2]

One day, while walking in the woods near Bennet's farm, Elizabeth found the name of Julia Scott written and fastened on a tree. At that moment, she thought she had really seen Julia's "ghost." Again, when Elizabeth paid Mammy Brown, a friend of Julia, her first visit, she immediately liked her for her affectionate and kind expressions about Julia.

Elizabeth knew that she could not be long absent from Julia. If she did not know whether Julia was well or ill, she could not help but feel "a pain peculiar to her affection" for Julia. When Julia was in trouble and seemingly out of reach of Elizabeth's affection, at those very times she was again restored to her place in Elizabeth's thoughts, but not in her affection, for her affection towards Julia always remained the same. Elizabeth wrote her: "Absence does not shake affection and friendship, rather does it strengthen them."[3]

Elizabeth was a rare kind of friend who felt the need to speak freely to Julia about religion. "Julia, you will not call me preacher or moralizer," she wrote. Religion does not limit the powers of affection, she told her; it alone can bind that cord over which neither circumstances, time nor death can have any power. Our Blessed Savior Himself sanctifies and approves in us all the endearing ties and connections of our existence. When Elizabeth wrote letters to some others, the words dropped so heavily that she could scarcely form them all. But when she began "Dear Julia," they flowed faster than the pen could write them. She asked: "Why do I tell you all this? How is it that never can I preserve any constancy in a letter to you, but always involuntarily express my thoughts as they arise?"[4]

Once, when Elizabeth was dozing over a volume of sermons ("such is the frailty of human nature," she explained), she remembered that she had not written Julia in ten days. In a moment, her eyes were open, thoughts awake, and every tender affection of her heart was in exercise. Another time, when she wanted to conclude a letter started the previous day but was called away by her father, brother, "Hub" and Colonel Giles in sequence, she finished the letter at seven the next morning. A letter that Elizabeth was writing Julia at eleven o'clock one evening was interrupted, but it was finished by her husband the next day with a note to Julia that Elizabeth had just given birth to a girl — later named Rebecca.

Elizabeth wrote Julia even when she was terribly busy. When her "darling Dick" was seriously ill a full week, she had not been in bed more than two hours any night. But she wrote the first free hour of the week to tell Julia everything. Sometimes, Elizabeth had to send letters off in haste, for if she did not conclude them that night, Julia would not receive them for several days. For some time, Elizabeth had allowed herself to lose the enjoyment she once had had in writing. Until Julia mentioned it, Elizabeth had underestimated the pain her silence would give Julia. When Elizabeth realized how long Julia had been expecting an answer to the "kind, tender proofs of her friendship," she admitted that, indeed, she had been long in arrears. As she closed that letter to Julia with many affectionate expressions, her tears flowed without restraint.

Elizabeth frequently included in her letters messages of affection from her family. On one occasion, when the family was together at her father's Health Establishment on Staten Island, Dr. Bayley entered the room at the moment Elizabeth was writing to Julia. Elizabeth quickly asked: "Have you any messages for my Julia?" Without hesitation, he replied: "Tell her I wish I had her at the Quarantine." The day he had seen Julia look so ill was, indeed, a day of sorrow for him. Elizabeth felt that if Julia would have asked his advice, "in the way that old friends ought to have done," she would have received it.[5]

Whimsically, Elizabeth wrote that her husband, William, was in love with Julia, with her house and with all that belonged to her. Elizabeth could not tell half of what he said about Julia's attentions to him and to his fellow travelers when they stopped to visit her. In return for Julia's kindness, William told Elizabeth that he meant to leave Julia (in case he died first) his ruby as a rich legacy. Once, he interrupted Elizabeth's letter writing to say:

> Do not forget to tell Julia that Miss Shipton sailed June 9, and that I sent her out like a Princess. The Captain was a smart little bachelor, with a handsome fortune, and a nephew to old Lady Fitch, so that I will not answer for the consequences before they get there.[6]

On one of William's visits to Julia's house, Elizabeth charged Julia to send her a kiss by William: "One, mind, no more, or you will be putting notions in the man's head." Then she added: "He will be with you next Thursday, I suppose, and then next Saturday, I hope with me who will make your one [kiss] many by all the rules of multiplication."[7] At another time, William sent Julia a kiss, and said that if she forgave him for not accepting the invitation for a family visit, she should have two. William had been constantly dreaming of her and remarked that a kiss had often occurred in the dreams — an unpropitious sign. So he feared that Julia was still angry with him and begged her, "for pity's sake to let the offenses of the old year pass with it."[8]

One evening, when William was "chained" at home, Elizabeth wrote Julia that he was poking the fire, scolding her for writing nonsense to Julia, "purreling" himself about his dream the night before, and wondering what he should do if he were a single man, adding that he believed his best plan was a voyage to the East Indies. Elizabeth was happy to say that Julia's box reached them safely, with such a "neat smart little affair," though she refused to promise Julia not to take off the bows — if Willy would let her take them off.

William was then writing quietly by her side, her "chicks" were in bed, and her father was smiling over a list of books which he had chosen to retain as one of the creditors in the Seton-Maitland bankruptcy. She reminded Julia that William was expecting her in time for the races. "Do not disappoint him, for he anticipates a great deal of pleasure."[9] William had wrapped a box for Julia which he marked W.E.S., and had included a picture which he thought she would like.

Elizabeth also enjoyed writing to Julia about the children who talked so fast that they confused her brain. Never a day passed without their saying something about "Aunt Scott," or Jack and Maria, Julia's children. Anna often said, "Mama, play you was Aunt Scott, and Bill and I, Jack and Maria." A drop of Aunt Scott's lavender on a little handkerchief, or a short story about John and Maria would delight Anna for an hour and keep her as quiet as a mouse.

William, the second child, also talked much of "Aunt Scott." He was a bouncer, and if permitted, would rule the house. While he was as sturdy and saucy as ever, Elizabeth was delighted to tell Julia that little William had an obedient and amiable disposition. Little Kate, then two years old, had on her first red shoes and was padding about delighting everybody's heart.

Elizabeth had often shared the cheerfulness of the blazing fire and the feeling tones of her piano with Julia. On one occasion when she was enjoying her stay on Long Island, she again invited Julia to come and be with her. She was sure that if Julia would taste the sweet breezes and the delights of the country as she was doing, she would be fully repaid for any trouble it might cost. She had already marked Julia's room. "Heaven grant that I may receive you and your son and daughter there with tranquility and health," she pleaded.[10]

On another occasion, when the time was approaching for Julia to visit Elizabeth in New York, Elizabeth had all in readiness: the bird cages were dressed, the flower pots replenished, the children all tip-top. She, herself, had just smoothed all the careworn wrinkles from her forehead, anticipating a day of perfect pleasure with Julia who was to accompany Dr. Bayley on his return to New York. Elizabeth was much chagrined when neither Julia nor her children had accompanied her father. On a similar occasion, when Julia had been expected with her brother, Samuel, Elizabeth wrote her: "But that is past, too, Julia, and when I shall have the opportunity of seeing either of you again is not to be thought of."[11]

After her father's death, when Elizabeth's world had just about crumbled, she wrote Julia: "Dear little Julia, I think if I would hold you once more to my heart, it would ease it of a heavy burden. Don't you think of seeing us in the spring."[12] Elizabeth repeated to Julia with a sigh (for she had no other relief) that unless Julia would come to her, she had not the smallest chance of seeing her.

In the past, whenever Julia invited Elizabeth to visit with her family in Philadelphia, this inability to work out a visit had been frequent because of Elizabeth's ever-changing family situation. On one such occasion while

Elizabeth's children were still very young and her family was growing, Julia's earnest invitation made Elizabeth smile. Having only Mammy Huler to assist her, Elizabeth was so entirely occupied with her family that she hardly had time to indulge a thought. Could Julia see the exact situation in which Elizabeth was at that moment, Elizabeth felt that she would acknowledge the impossibility of visiting her. If she retired one moment, Elizabeth heard a half dozen voices calling "sister" or "mama." She answered Julia:

> Suppose you had a nurseling and a half a dozen besides; suppose yourself providing and arranging for my family, and suppose yourself a teacher of reading, writing, sewing, etc., for I devote the whole morning, that is, from ten until two to my three girls [her sisters-in-law, Charlotte, Mary and Rebecca].[13]

Their going to school through snow and wet would give Elizabeth more trouble, she knew, than keeping them at home. She had tried the latter strategy for one week, and thus far, it had been only a pleasure.

Sometime later, when Julia had offered the same invitation to visit her, Elizabeth wrote:

> Dear little soul, you who can bear no exertions even in common causes, require your friend with all her weights and measures to leave home, physicians and a thousand etceteras to take a journey through roads almost impassable, and to return when they certainly must be worse! You might as well say, "Come, friend, we will make a jaunt to the moon!"[14]

About a year had passed when Elizabeth had to write Julia again to tell her that the projected visit to her, "like all other schemes that go against the stream must be deferred." How Elizabeth could leave home at any time was not easy to conceive! At that writing, she had in addition to her own charges her sister-in-law Eliza Maitland's infant, and its wet nurse during the winter change. Overburdened with duties and without a servant, she had to set her own table, and do all the work of a servant-man except cleaning knives.

Although Elizabeth's friendship with Julia entailed many disappointments, her love for her friend never diminished. Julia, healthy, cheerful, amusing herself and receiving the caresses of her friends was always "dear Julia." Elizabeth could resign herself at not being with her, pursue her work without regret, and think it was for the best. But, Julia in trouble or suffering of any kind touched every nerve of Elizabeth's heart. Then, feeling an exclusive right to be with her friend, she could fly over mountains to support her aching heart. Not long after her marriage to William Seton, Elizabeth had written her friend, Eliza Sadler, about Julia:

> Julia is a little vain shadow and never interests me but when she is in sickness or sorrow — then I fly to her, hold her in my bosom till the storm is past, and only care enough for her to hold the chain together until it comes round again.[15]

Two years later, Elizabeth again wrote Eliza that Fate had ordered the husband of "poor little Julia Scott to the regions of peace." On that occasion, during the excess of Julia's sorrow, Elizabeth never left her night or day. The scenes of terror she had gone through neither Eliza nor anyone could conceive.

Many times, Elizabeth had been sufficiently unhappy at not being able to see Julia, but after she received Julia's letters filled with melancholy impressions, images too painful to dwell on, Elizabeth experienced even greater sorrow and anxiety. If she could be allowed the comfort of being with Julia in her afflictions, she would willingly quit home and all its charms with only the privilege of bringing her "little nurseling" with her. To see Julia's letter wet with tears was too much for Elizabeth. She wrote her:

> If it was possible to love you more than I did, how much nearer would it now draw you to my heart to find you in sorrow and inquietude, struggling with all the vexations and cares of a mind oppressed.[16]

Elizabeth seemed never to relax in her constant concern over Julia's dejected spirits. "Are you well? Are you happy?" she inquired. On numerous occasions, Elizabeth wrote her that their mutual friend, Colonel Giles, had frightened the Setons. He asked William continually: "Has Mrs. Seton heard from her friend?" Twice, woe-begone, he had paid the Setons a visit and complained that Julia had not written to any of her friends. Elizabeth felt that Julia was unfair in not writing to Colonel Giles, a faithful friend. From her own experience, Elizabeth hoped that with time Julia's afflictions would be alleviated, and that the focus on her own misfortunes would shift to those of her friends.

Fearing that sorrow had gained too much control over Julia's mind, Elizabeth made every effort to pull her out of her depression. In her gloomy state, neither the fine weather, nor spring, nor exercise could give her more than partial relief. Elizabeth was anxious that Julia not trifle or delay asking her physician's advice when it was necessary — even for a trivial matter. She had been accustomed to care and attention, and she must still use the good that was in her power. Elizabeth knew Julia well. She had known Julia to write to her father or brother in the morning on the most melancholy subjects, and in the afternoon dress, go visiting, and be the most cheerful of the company.

Julia was not born to be unhappy, or heaven would never have given her such a brother as Samuel, "who must ever be the most proper and effectual comforter of her heart," Elizabeth wrote her. Besides, her children, Maria and John, were sufficient to tie her to this life which she seemed careless of possessing, but which was so necessary to their future happiness. Maria was at an age that would soon supply a thousand sources of enjoyment.

> Think what is the difference to her, if you preserve your health or lose it. You never knew the want of a mother's tender care, or you would tremble that your child should ever want it.[17]

In an effort to soothe and comfort Julia, from time to time, Elizabeth wrote about her own suffering. She thought that to compare one's burdens with the cares of others sometimes lessened one's personal sorrows. In her siege of sorrows, Elizabeth felt that she had cause to weep from Monday to Saturday. When she looked back on the first four years of her married life, she was filled with anguish and could have cried like a child at the thought of the innocent and past pleasures that she had enjoyed, though she never knew their value. She could not help longing again for that rest which she had never known but in her Wall Street home.

It appeared to Elizabeth, then, that she was not to be herself again. "Death, or bread and water, would be a happy prospect in comparison," she wrote Julia. She was not the lively animated Betsy Bayley, but the softened matron with traces of care and anxiety on her brow. "You can scarcely imagine one more lonely than I," she told Julia. Never in her

life had she suffered so much from the anticipation of evil —
a source of uneasiness Elizabeth never liked to indulge.

William himself had been long ill with the prevailing fever. Though he had but a slight attack, it was sufficient to terrify Elizabeth, particularly since they were at Bloomingdale (then on the outskirts of New York) without an attending physician. Besides, William's disposition was of the kind that wrapped its grief in the still of despair. Then, when it was learned that William's business affairs had failed, Elizabeth took some comfort in writing letters to his creditors on his behalf — a task which would have caused him a great deal of trouble. Elizabeth felt that knowing the whys and wherefores of his business failure made her a better companion for him. In four weeks, her pen had been scarcely out of her hand "except for sleep or rather to weep." She had much more of the latter than the former, she told Julia. In addition, her husband's friends — Stone, Ogden and "everyone" — had abandoned him and she was most truly his all.

Elizabeth also mentioned to Julia Scott the painful changes in her home situation. Never alone, without leisure hours and caring less than ever for the world and its pleasures, Elizabeth was sure that their house was to be declared bankrupt, or that William must go to prison. Besides, his health was declining so rapidly that there could be no hope of his recovery, "in the view of mortal hopes." Elizabeth's last letter to Julia, written the day before she set sail for Leghorn, Italy, with William for the recovery of his health, seemed to express the ultimate of her sufferings. In the month of August she had weaned a sick baby, had broken up housekeeping and ever since had been in hourly expectation of embarking for Leghorn.

Nor was Elizabeth herself free from physical pain. For several months while attempting to care for her family, she suffered pain in her back all day and in her side at night. At times, even while she was writing to Julia, she was in pain, once with a boil on her arm. On another occasion, she could have told her a great deal about her children, but her thumb was bound up with a poultice, and she wrote with difficulty.

When Richard, her third child, was born, Elizabeth was so terribly ill that her father could scarcely perform his medical task. Every exertion was necessary to save her life. From strain, she had been almost blind in her better eye. Her little son was for some hours thought past hope; she herself came within one more pain of death. She truly felt that her father had given Richard the breath of life, for when the child neither breathed nor moved, Dr. Bayley went on his knees and, placing his mouth to the child's lips, forcibly blew breath into his lungs. At her father's death, Elizabeth suffered so much from aches of her teeth and temples that she felt she had been really stupefied. "Therefore," she wrote Julia:

> When you sit nursing and thoughtful about your crosses and accidents, turn your mind to your friend and view the changes of the last few years in my lot; and when you have traced it to the present period, figure to yourself Mr. Barrett Kittlet as the winder-up of bankrupts, sitting in our library taking inventory of our furniture, goods, etc.[18]

Elizabeth felt that it was all in vain to grieve over her sorrows. Rather, a melancholy satisfaction in being able to sustain herself and reconcile every decree of fate for William's sake came over her. Like Julia she, too, was a mother; she was far from being so selfish as to wish to leave her charges while her care was required. "But the knot of oak," as William called her, told Julia that she had not suffered that much inconvenience although her mind was sufficiently troubled about the future. Elizabeth assured Julia that small as her portion of happiness might appear to her, she had no less than any other person who had suffered a reverse of family affairs. "So you see, dear Julia, the debt we pay for this beautiful creation, and the many enjoyments of this life are to be borne in some degree by us all."[19]

Elizabeth tried to keep up courage by counting her blessings. Nothing but the smiles and health of her children could have saved her from melancholy. She had the enjoyment of books, music, walking, the piano, and a cribbage party for William. When it was decided that she and her children should remain all summer with her father on Staten Island, she took pleasure that they had an upper balcony which commanded a view fifty miles beyond Sandy Hook. William came and spent four days of the week with her; her father very seldom left the house but to visit vessels, and the children were perfectly wild with the country.

When she had once more returned to her home on State Street, she doubly enjoyed its "sweet comforts," although in the week past, with as cheerful a countenance as Julia had ever seen, Elizabeth had watched and attended the street door to keep out the sheriff's officers. Her strength of mind seemed to increase with the storm in her daily life. "But acting well our part in present difficulties was the only way to insure the peace of futurity," she wrote Julia.

Contrary to Julia's search for happiness in the pleasures of this world, Elizabeth viewed the world as a ship passage to her eternal home, and herself a passenger. "I have as bright a hope, and faith as strong as ever animated a mortal," she wrote. Without the prospect of heaven, this life would be a scene of confusion and vexation, Elizabeth thought. She found in it no enjoyment so great that it would induce her to remain here one moment longer. Even as the mother of her children she would not stay, if she were sure they would not be deprived of the protection of their father.

Elizabeth wanted Julia to think of death. Pain and a thousand nameless anxieties reminded her continually of that hour in which the soul wavers between its future home and the present. She recalled for Julia two deaths that she had witnessed. While attending the fortnight death-struggle of her sister-in-law, Mary Hoffman Seton, and witnessing the sorrow of James Seton, her brother-in-law, Elizabeth found herself overpowered, fainting and extremely weak. She told Julia that her sister-in-law died a dreadful death, the circumstances and scenes of which could never be effaced from her imagination. They had one powerful effect on her — that of making her yet more anxious and careful in preparing for her own hour of death.

In contrast, Mammy Huler, the second mother of Elizabeth's children, was literally "born anew." She died without a struggle or groan, as a child composed to rest in the arms of its parents and certain of a secure awakening:

> Oh, if you could have witnessed in her the comforts and consolations of a humble soul seeking a refuge of a Redeemer, you would teach your children that to know and love Him is the Only Good.[20]

What Elizabeth really wished for Julia and her children was heaven's blessings. The only word which approached that meaning was *peace*. "Were it in my lot to speak peace to your afflicted heart!" she prayed. Nature would demand struggles of Julia, but heaven would restore her to peace. This was what Elizabeth desired for herself, and hoped that one day they might share together. "O Julia," she wrote her, "if my wishes or exertions could gain your peace, you would enjoy it in its most perfect state."[21]

To keep the thought of heaven ever before her was the prayer of Elizabeth's heart, "and let it be the prayer of yours," she begged Julia. Yet in all her repeated pleadings with Julia to reflect on the future life and eternity, Elizabeth realized that, perhaps, in God's searching eye, Julia was surer of possessing heaven than herself who so often begged it for Julia.

The above account does not exhaust the tenderness of Elizabeth's friendship with Julia Scott, nor Julia's response to Elizabeth's love. After Elizabeth's conversion to Catholicism, although she did not share Elizabeth's religious beliefs, Julia remained her faithful friend — a friend for every need which Elizabeth expressed to her. When she heard of Elizabeth's hardships and impoverishment in New York after William's death, Julia offered her money. She sent her $200 annually for Anna's education and dancing lessons, but at times, Elizabeth was forced to use the money for more pressing needs.

Just before Elizabeth left New York for Baltimore, she wrote Julia:

> Of all the many attachments I have had, you are the only one on earth to whom my heart turns in the simple unrepressed warmth of confiding love. Every other is shackled with hesitations, doubts, calculations — so contradictory to my nature.[22]

Julia's generosity toward Elizabeth and her children continued through the years. While they were in Baltimore and later in Emmitsburg, Julia sent them clothes and money, and personal gifts to Anna to allow her some independence. Feeling the pinch of poverty, Elizabeth accepted Julia's benefactions, sometimes reluctantly but always with a grateful heart. Julia's continuous money gifts were used, at times, for "little comforts" for Anna on a trip to Baltimore, and for Catherine Josephine's visit with friends. They were also used to outfit William and Richard as they set out in search of a life-career.

Julia's boundless generosity extended beyond Emmitsburg to the Sisters at the orphanage in Philadelphia when they could not pay the bills incurred for the orphans. Nor was she less generous in little Rebecca's case when the child travelled to Philadelphia to visit Dr. Physick, a specialist, in hope of a cure for her lame leg.

As the years rolled by, to allay Julia's fears and concern about her happiness and her children's welfare, Elizabeth invited Julia to Saint Joseph's Valley to come and see for herself Elizabeth's joy and contentment as mother to her children, to her students at Saint Joseph's Academy, and to all the community of Sisters of Charity which she had founded. Julia's only visit to Saint Joseph's in thirteen years was a short one. But during all these years, Elizabeth had kept Julia constantly in her heart.

In New York while maintaining a close friendship with Julia Scott, much her senior in years, Elizabeth was at the same time nurturing the friendship of Cecilia Seton, not yet in her teens.

Portrait of Elizabeth Seton by Favret de St-Mesmin, French immigrant, New York, 1796.

The famed Doctor Richard Bayley, surgeon. Father of Elizabeth Ann Seton.

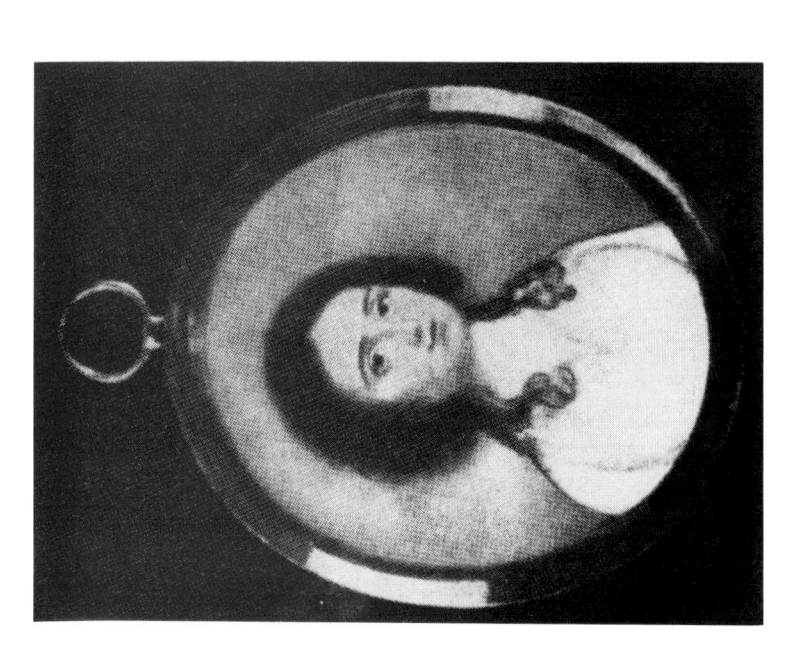

Early portraits of Elizabeth Ann Seton and her husband-friend, William Magee Seton.

Elizabeth Seton. Saint-Mesmin miniature.

A later portrait of William Magee Seton, husband of Elizabeth Ann Seton.

The Lazaretto in Leghorn, Italy where Elizabeth and William Seton were held in quarantine for one month.

Antonio Filicchi, friend and sponsor of Elizabeth Ann Seton, Leghorn, Italy.

Amabilia Filicchi, wife of Antonio Filicchi. Befriended Elizabeth Seton in Leghorn, Italy.

Mary Cowper Filicchi, wife of Filippo Filicchi. Befriended Elizabeth Seton in Leghorn, Italy. Archives Saint Joseph's Provincial House, Emmitsburg, Maryland.

Filippo Filicchi, friend and business associate of William Seton, holding his testimonial as United States Consul in Leghorn (Livorno), Italy.

Facsimile Autograph Letter of Elizabeth to Antonio Filicchi. Preserved in the Filicchi archives, Leghorn, Italy.

The Paca Street House, Baltimore, Maryland, where Elizabeth Seton first started her school.

A view of the Stone House in its original location. Archives Saint Joseph's Provincial House, Emmitsburg, Maryland.

Elizabeth Ann Seton in Saint Joseph's Valley by Sister Fides Glass, S.C., Greensburg, Pennsylvania.

An Early View of the White House, Emmitsburg, Maryland.

The Reverend Simon Gabriel Bruté, Elizabeth Seton's friend and spiritual director of her community in Emmitsburg, Maryland.

Mortuary Chapel and Cemetery, Emmitsburg, Maryland.

Robert Goodloe Harper (1765-1825), Major General in the service of the United States. Befriended Elizabeth Ann Seton in Emmitsburg, Maryland.

The Shrine of St. Elizabeth Ann Seton at 8 State Street on the southern tip of Manhattan, overlooking New York Harbor. Elizabeth Seton and her family lived here from 1801 to 1803.

CHAPTER 8

CECILIA SETON:
My Spiritual Half And Inseparable Friend

As mistress of the Seton household after the death of the elder Mr. Seton, Elizabeth would be given charge of her young sisters-in-law: Rebecca, Harriet and Cecilia. From their first meeting, she would have a special fondness for Cecilia, the youngest of the Seton girls. In entering the Catholic Church at the age of fifteen, Cecilia, in the company of Elizabeth, would also go through persecution, hardships and sickness. United in this common bond, the two became close friends.

Cecilia was still very young when Elizabeth began teaching her about God. Only the knowledge of God could fill her heart with that peace and joy which nothing on earth could disturb. For those who keep their hearts fixed on Him, and who try with all their souls to please Him, God has prepared a place of everlasting joy, she instructed Cecilia. "When He calls them, 'come up hither', they will fly with joy to their heavenly home."[1] In heaven, they would never be separated, never be weary, but would rejoice always before His throne.

While Elizabeth, not yet converted to Catholicism, had been preparing to depart for Leghorn, Italy, she had worried about Cecilia's spiritual well-being even though she had left her with "dearest friends and under God's protecting care." She urged her to fulfill "the habitual observance of the Christian life she had so early begun," and to make for herself a few particular rules for carrying out her sacred duty to God, no matter what the obstacles. Even those who acted differently from her steady way would not lessen their esteem of her. As a last word to Cecilia before setting sail for Leghorn, Elizabeth wrote her: "Rejoice to bear your share in the cross which is our passport and seal to the kingdom of our Redeemer."[2]

Following her return to New York from Leghorn, Elizabeth rejoiced to find that Cecilia, despite many hardships, was still her sister in spirit and in nature. She told Cecilia that when she prayed for herself she never said *me* anymore, but always *us*. One thing she knew for sure: she loved her more than herself, more than all her children. In fact, Cecilia was her dearest child.

During the time that Cecilia lived with her Protestant relatives, Elizabeth longed heart and soul to see her. Without her the days seemed long and tedious; with her a day would, indeed, be a "gala day." To be near Cecilia, Elizabeth wished she could be a chair, or anything, in order to pass some hours with her. She wanted to lean her wearied head on Cecilia's shoulder or have a good frolic with her. "What a sweet day to me," she exclaimed.[3]

One afternoon when Elizabeth was more alone than usual and her heart was calling out for Cecilia, she felt that she had dwelt on her too much. As she recounted this experience to Cecilia she added somewhat wryly: "But hush, covetous nature." If the two of them could pass a day or a night together, she would repeat to her the story of Christ's suffering and anguish, "the Christ who chose them for His companions from the cradle to the grave."

About a month after Elizabeth, now a Catholic, had received the sacrament of Confirmation, Cecilia startled many of her relatives by becoming a Catholic. She had been received by the Rev. Michael Hurley at Saint Peter's Church in New York City on June 20, 1806. When her relatives (the Setons, Farquhars, and Wilkes) had learned of her conversion, in their violent anger they began to persecute both her and Elizabeth. Elizabeth wrote Antonio Filicchi, then in Leghorn, how Cecilia had been followed "by the most abusive letters and charges against the Faith, Bigotry, superstition, wicked Priests, etc."[4] The ridicule affected Cecilia as little as it did Elizabeth; the real distress, she told Antonio, was in hearing their Faith misrepresented and in experiencing with grief the darkness of those who despised it.

In a family meeting, the relatives resolved that if Cecilia persevered in the Catholic faith they would consider themselves individually bound never to speak to her nor to Elizabeth, and never again to allow Cecilia to enter their houses. If she did not consent to their wishes they threatened to send her from the country. Elizabeth, too, should be turned out a beggar with her children. They said "many other nonsenses not worth mentioning," Elizabeth told Antonio.

Supported by Elizabeth during this period of persecution, Cecilia, very early in the morning of the day she would be turned out of her Protestant relatives' house, quietly tied up her clothes in a bundle and went to live with Elizabeth. The relatives' objections were so many that Elizabeth became concerned not only for Cecilia's future, but also for the future of her own "little girls," if God should take her from this life. As a mother, she felt it her responsibility not to trust them to so dangerous a situation. To offset the harsh treatment of the relatives, Elizabeth wrote encouragingly to Cecilia: "when your wearied heart sinks and does not feel God's immediate presence, then tho' hidden, He is nearest."[5] She wrote Antonio that "little Cecilia" was trying to be a saint. "Saint Cecilia, Saint Delia, handsome American names, should it be so."

Cecila was not long with Elizabeth when at the death of Mary Hoffman Seton, Cecilia's brother, the now widowed James immediately took Cecilia to his home where she would have the charge of his eight children, though he was naturally fearful of the effect that Cecilia's Catholic influence would have on the children. Elizabeth noted to Julia Scott: "Her poor brother finds his greatest consolation in her faithful and unwearied attentions to himself and his children; therefore, my deprivation is easily reconciled having many comforts he has not."[6]

It was not long until the painful wounds suffered by Cecilia at her conversion were torn open again. The governess of the family endeavored to persuade James Seton that Cecilia was instilling the principles of the Catholic faith in his eldest daughter. The incident once more made both Cecilia and Elizabeth the burning topic of the relatives' conversation. This trial affected Cecilia so severely that Elizabeth felt it would probably soon put an end to her since she was already suffering from chest pains.

Elizabeth took this opportunity to tell Cecilia that from past experience, she knew for sure that Cecilia would be thankful for the privilege of suffering for God. As the antidote to the discord surrounding her, Elizabeth always whispered Jesus' name of love and invited Cecilia to do the same in her sufferings. She related to her how one morning she awoke at five o'clock rejoicing as she prepared herself for Mass. Her heart had beaten "true to love" that morning when the clock struck seven and she was on her knees before

Father Hurley to receive Jesus in the Blessed Sacrament, "the dearest consolation their world can afford."

Frequently, in her dreams, Elizabeth was with Jesus. One morning after a weary night when several of her household were ill, Elizabeth recounted to Cecilia how in a dream she accompanied Jesus through the streets of Jerusalem all that night. On another occasion she dreamed that she was holding the Blessed Host close to her heart, making earnest acts of adoration and love which were mixed with the fear of losing heaven, when suddenly a quantity of almonds and raisins were thrown in her lap. At that moment Elizabeth awakened from her dream. She wrote Cecilia: "You know how fond I am of them, earthly affections...."[7]

Despite God's bounteous goodness to her, Elizabeth often thought of herself as rejected. In this continual change of interior disposition, she told Cecilia that she, too, walked in darkness and often went astray. She desired, yet knew not how to desire. She loved, yet knew not how to love, nor how to find what she loved. To love God above all things was Elizabeth's most cherished desire, yet she felt it was above the reach and strength of nature. Then, as she remembered God's immediate presence, she whispered to Him: "But I am inexcusable, if I do not love Thee, for Thou grantest Thy love to all who desire or ask it."[8]

To overcome these moments of desolation and to restore the love of Jesus in her heart, Elizabeth frequented the Sacrament of Reconciliation, i.e. Confession. She wrote Cecilia:

> When our corrupted nature overpowers, when we are sick of ourselves weakened on all sides, discouraged with repeated relapses, wearied with sin and sorrow, we gently, sweetly lay the whole account at His feet, reconciled and encouraged by His appointed representative [the priest], yet trembling and conscious of our imperfect dispositions, we draw near the Sacred Fountain.[9]

When she had once more received Jesus at His holy altar, Elizabeth told Cecilia, her soul was again at peace.

Elizabeth loved to kneel with Cecilia at Holy Communion to share her peace and the anticipated joy of eternity. Once, despite the separation of many miles, Elizabeth's soul felt this joy in unison with Cecilia's as their "hearts burned within" them. Elizabeth later told Cecilia that it was the joy of tears such as they had experienced together when once before they had adored in His presence. Although they daily offered each other to God, Elizabeth felt that Cecilia should warn Elizabeth not to love her *too much*, lest she become possessive of her. But as Elizabeth recalled Cecilia's present hostile environment and her uncertain future prospects, she remarked that both of them should be thankful for their past happiness and leave all to God's will with a peaceful resignation.

To quell Cecilia's fears about being left behind should Elizabeth have to leave New York, Elizabeth assured Cecilia that she could never leave her alone in dejection and adversity. "Death alone can take your sister from you," she wrote, "while there is the least probability you may want her sheltering heart."[10]

Like Cecilia, Elizabeth, too, was a "prisoner of the Lord," a prisoner of Protestant relatives. She had been fighting her own feelings so long that she feared she had brought Cecilia only pain instead of cheerfulness and consolation. As long as Cecilia suffered, so did Elizabeth. Her eyes smarted and her heart ached. Then, putting her confidence in Him "who had strengthened the bond between them," Elizabeth exclaimed: "Shall we get out of this stormy ocean [the persecutions] and rest at his feet? Heavenly thought!"[11]

It was a "little mystery" to Elizabeth how Cecilia's heart could be so long "in the ditch" when God was every moment looking at her. Elizabeth was "very, very earnest" that Cecilia do her part to get rid of depression. She wondered whether Cecilia remembered the last morning when the two of them saw Fr. Hurley at Mass and whether she had noticed how earnestly he had said to them: *"Sursum Corda"* ["Lift up your hearts"]. These words had made so strong an impression on Elizabeth at the time that they often echoed in her when her own depression made her deaf to every other remembrance.

From experience, Elizabeth knew that when the heart was totally God's, pain and sorrow were easier and even contained a secret joy. "All that God asks of us is the heart," she wrote, "Nor can there be a more perfectly acceptable offering to Him than a heart feeble but willing as His own in our human nature once has been."[12]

Elizabeth counselled Cecilia to gently put into God's hands, with simplicity of heart, the most innocent and dearest joys of one's life. She wanted her to reflect for a moment how precious the constant aspirations of her "little Virgin heart" must be to its Master, and then she would not be sad a moment at any privation. As a special offering to Him, Elizabeth encouraged her not to neglect her journal. "Mine is going on," she mentioned.

Mindful of the importance of prayer in one's life, Elizabeth quoted to Cecilia the command of Christ — "pray always."[13] "We must pray literally without ceasing — without ceasing," she emphasized, "in every occurrence and employment of our lives." She explained that what is meant is the prayer of the heart which, independent of place or situation, is rather a habit of lifting up the heart to God at every opportunity. She wanted Cecilia to appeal to Him who saw her heart and knew how much she would prefer to devote every hour of her day to Him. She told her that God by secret and unknown ways communicates Himself to us in such a manner that in the midst of activities His presence is felt. The sacrifices she made while living with her brother,

James Seton, and caring for his children as a ministering angel, were as welcome to "our dear Lord" as if she had been adoring at His altar.

Elizabeth felt that it was the Mother of God who could best teach Cecilia this prayer of the heart. Mostly for her own consolation, Elizabeth mentioned to her that God often separates His servants from whatever they love most so that He Himself may take its place in their hearts — "divesting us of everything else that we may be alone with Him and thereby enjoy unutterable peace."[14]

With Christ continually in her heart, Cecilia would find peace. "How silly," Elizabeth wrote her, "to set your little brain to work and threaten it with a storm that may never come." If, however, the storm of added suffering feared by Cecilia should befall her, Elizabeth predicted that it would drive her still further into her interior castle and point out to her the path of future peace.[15]

To deepen Cecilia in the meaning of suffering, Elizabeth suggested that she read *The Sufferings of Our Lord Jesus Christ* by Thomas of Jesus (De Andrada), a book of meditations on the passion of Christ. This book had taken the place of all her other reading and of almost all other prayers. Elizabeth hoped that it would be for Cecilia, too, a source of continual prayer.

Turning her thoughts to their eternal reward, Elizabeth affirmed to Cecilia that "death and eternity are the only certainty." "Cecy," she said, "what should we fear? Heaven is for us. What should be against us? Old Lucifer cannot gain a step but what we give him."[16] Still Elizabeth hoped that she might one day enjoy Cecilia's society, even in this world.

Contrary to her own and Elizabeth's wishes, Cecilia's fears of losing Elizabeth became a reality. While Elizabeth prepared to leave New York for Paca Street in Baltimore,

Cecilia, in poor health, was forced to remain in New York. Her spiritual director, the Rev. Anthony Kohlman, S.J., concerned about her health, advised her to await the manifest will of God in her desire to live in religious seclusion. Cecilia did not anticipate "a life of ease and pleasure," she wrote, "but a life of penance and humiliation."

At New York Harbor, Elizabeth and her three daughters boarded the *Grand Sachem*, a packet, on June 9, 1808. They sailed down along the Atlantic seaboard and arrived in Baltimore one week later. En route, Elizabeth kept an account of her journey for Cecilia. As she passed the lighthouse thirty miles from New York, she wrote her that with "the firmament of heaven so bright" all the fatigue and weariness of mind and body were passed; the cheering sea-breezes and merry sailors would drive care away, indeed, if she had the company of the "five dearest beings who bade adieu in the little room," as she left.

Several days later, as Elizabeth and the girls were flying up the Chesapeake, the glorious setting sun reminded Elizabeth of how she and Cecilia said together the *Miserere*, their evening prayer. Elizabeth and her girls finally arrived in Baltimore Bay in the rain on June 16, the feast of Corpus Christi. A carriage waited to convey them to the seminary for the consecration of Fr. DuBourg's chapel. "Your imagination can never conceive the splendor — the glory of the scene," she wrote Cecilia as she recalled the organ's solemn peal and the burst of the choir.

Surrounded by love and the gracious hospitality of Fr. DuBourg's mother and his sister's family, Elizabeth longed for Cecilia whose uppermost wish of her heart was to be in Baltimore. A year later, through the intercession of Bishop Carroll, Elizabeth would once again enjoy Cecilia's company. Meanwhile, the nearly invalid Cecilia wrote her:

> When I commence writing to you, I know not how to stop and have so much to say, I know not where to begin. Will my love for you be ever the same? . . . Heaven forbid it should be other than it is. Our ties are too closely united with our love for Him.[17]

During the year of waiting, Elizabeth was preparing for Cecilia's arrival. Anna, Elizabeth's daughter, Aglaé and Celanine, Fr. DuBourg's nieces, among others, were eager to see their "Aunt Cecilia." Besides, plans were being made to establish the school and convent in Emmitsburg, a distance of fifty miles from Baltimore[18] where they could breathe the country air. When it was finally decided that Cecilia would join Elizabeth, the latter wrote her:

> I cannot but expect you with joy such as you alone can believe who know how much my happiness is connected with yours. Do not bring any other clothes but a black gown. Keep your heart in peace and as composed as possible in parting with so many most dear to you.[19]

Despite the alarming symptoms which Cecilia's health began to show early in the spring of 1809, her brother, Samuel, wrote Elizabeth on May 25 that all arrangements were complete. He and their sister, Harriet, would accompany Cecilia to Baltimore. Harriet, who had cared for Cecilia in her illness (tuberculosis), wanted to see her safely in Elizabeth's arms. The little group sailed from New York on the first of June and arrived at Paca Street on June 12.

Within ten days, on June 21, the feast of Saint Aloysius, Elizabeth, her two sisters-in-law, her daughter Anna, and Sister Maria Murphy set out in a covered wagon for the mountains in Emmitsburg hoping to give Cecilia the benefit of purer air. With a joyful heart, Elizabeth wrote Father DuBourg in Baltimore an account of the journey:

> Your turnpike is a rough one; we were obliged to walk the horses all the way, and have walked ourselves, all except Cecilia, nearly half the time: this morning four miles and a half before breakfast. The dear patient [Cecilia] was greatly amused at the procession, and all the natives astonished as we went before the carriage.[20]

Not finding the farmhouse ready for them, Elizabeth and her group continued their trek to the mountaintop across the road and were graciously offered hospitality by the Rev. John DuBois, founder of Mount Saint Mary's College. They occupied the small cottage used as a retreat house by the Sulpician Fathers and remained there until the end of July 1809. During their stay, Cecilia's health had only temporarily improved. When they moved to the "Stone House" on the Fleming farm, she was admitted as a Sister to Elizabeth's growing community of Sisters of Charity.

But only several months later, on March 1, 1810, Cecilia wrote Fr. Pierre Babade who had befriended her in Baltimore: "With a cheerful heart I feel myself every day get weaker, and feel happy in the idea that a few weeks must end it all."[21] With death and eternity ever before her, Cecilia drew strength from her association with Elizabeth and their friendship in the Lord. About the middle of April, on the advice of a physician for a change of air and better medical opportunities, Sr. Cecilia Seton was conveyed to Baltimore by Elizabeth Seton. They were accompanied by Anna and Sr. Susan.

Comforted by the Holy Communion she had received, Cecilia drew her last breath in Baltimore on April 29, 1810.

She was the admiration of all who knew her. The Mass of the Resurrection was celebrated for her in St. Mary's chapel in Baltimore. After the ceremony, Mother Seton with the Rev. Mr. Clorivière, a cleric, and Sr. Susan, returned to Emmitsburg with Cecilia's remains. They were laid to rest in the Sisters' cemetery in Saint Joseph's Valley, as the site of the Fleming farm was renamed.

Elizabeth Seton later wrote her friend, Eliza Sadler:

> Dearest Harriet[22] and my angel Cecil sleep in the wood close beside me. The children and many of our good sisters to whom they were much attached have planted their graves with wild flowers, and the little inclosure which contains them is the dearest spot to me on earth. I do not miss them half as much as you would think, as according to my *mad notions*, it seems as if they are always around me.[23]

Through the years, two other of her early friends, namely, Catherine Dupleix and Eliza Sadler, also remained faithful to Elizabeth Seton. An account of this friendship follows.

CHAPTER 9

Catherine Dupleix and Eliza Sadler
My Never Failing New York Friends

After Elizabeth Seton became a Catholic in 1805, she moved to Paca Street in Baltimore in 1808, to found a religious community of teaching sisters. She then permanently established "Saint Joseph's Academy" and "The Sisters of Charity of Saint Joseph's" in Emmitsburg. Despite all these intense activities, her close friendship with Catherine Dupleix and Eliza Sadler seems to have never wavered.

During their early friendship in New York society, Elizabeth and her friends, "Dué" and "Sad" as she had nicknamed them, took an active part in the Widows' Society, in which Elizabeth was for a time the treasurer. Such was their devotion to the relief of the poor that on their errands of mercy, Elizabeth, her sister-in-law Rebecca, Dué and Sad were called "Protestant Sisters of Charity." Ironically, after the Setons were forced to file bankruptcy at the failure of the Seton-Maitland shipping interests, Elizabeth, in poverty and need, had to turn to the Widow's Society for help.

During her four-year struggle in New York to support herself and her children, and to find the true faith, many of her former friends grew tired of her doubts, hesitancies and scruples, and abandoned her. But Catherine Dupleix and Eliza Sadler remained loyal in defending her against her former friends turned enemies. As the years rolled by, their mutual affection deepened. Elizabeth, separated from them so many years, longed to see them and to put her children in their arms once more. She wished very much to show them the beautiful mountain facing Saint Joseph's Valley in Emmitsburg — the mountain which symbolized her Sisterhood's dedication to Christ and His children. Their coming to Saint Joseph's would fulfill one of Elizabeth's greatest wishes, and give her more happiness than she dared look for in ordinary life. Such was the closeness of their friendship that when Elizabeth had time to write to only one of them, a single letter had to carry her "tenderest remembrances" to both.

* * *

While living on Baltimore's Paca Street in dire poverty and at a distance from all those "allied by natural affection" to her, Elizabeth wrote Dué that her soul seemed to cry out after her as its "dearest sister." Elizabeth begged her never to think for a minute that time, absence or above all, Dué's carelessness in writing, would change even in one degree a friendship which for so many years had been a part of Elizabeth's heart. Elizabeth read a letter just received from Dué with "sweet delight" in that God gave them a heart to love each other without restraints, calculations or fears of saying too much or too little.

Elizabeth wanted Dué to write her "close and small," and to tell her what was in her heart, where she was, and how she was doing. In later years, when Elizabeth had sent her religious sisters to open an orphanage in New York, she expressed joy that Dué loved Sister Margaret George: "a heart so truly made to be loved; I am sure she will not disappoint you."[1] Knowing Dué's dislike for letter writing, Elizabeth suggested that Dué make Sister Margaret George her clerk. "She is swift with her pen and always delighted to help anyone — how much more one as loved as you are," she wrote.[2]

Elizabeth particularly enjoyed writing Dué about her children who considered Dué one of their mother's unchanging friends. From Paca Street, Elizabeth wrote that she had asked "impudent Ann" who was standing by her side what she should say to Dué for her. Ann answered by "gabbling a mess of French compliments but ended them in plain English" with the remark that she longed for the moment of seeing Dué again. Elizabeth added that Bill then was the "drollest creature" Dué ever could imagine, always full of fun, which he loved much better than his grammar. When he and Dick were saying what they would do if they had a fifty-mile race to run, Dick said: "For my part, I would go right up to the clouds." But Bill said: "I would not. I would go straight to Ireland and whip up Dué on my back and she would be here in a jiffy."[3]

On Rebecca's sixth birthday, Elizabeth recalled for Dué what a memorable day the child's birth was for both of them: "What did you not suffer for me, my Dué, on that day. You were the first person who cherished and nursed the dear little being."[4] She recounted the incident when recently Rebecca was speaking of Dué to her companions and called her, "my dearest Dué." One of them asked: "Who is Dué?" Rebecca, with a toss of her head, quite affronted that they did not know her Dué, answered: "She is a lady whom I love very much and wish she was here."[5] That letter closed with kisses from the heart to Dué on this spot.

While Dué was in Ireland, Elizabeth heard the worst accounts of her health. She wrote Sad about it: "How hard it is to say, the soul we love may be in the world of worlds before we know it."[6] Elizabeth wanted Dué to take care of herself for their sakes, too, for the five "dear ones" (Elizabeth's children) whom she loved, and to come to them if anything should happen to her. If Elizabeth could but share her comforts with Dué or share Dué's pain with her at Saint Joseph's — "my friend," she wrote, "the pen is silent when the heart says too much."[7] But Dué's sufferings, like Elizabeth's, would at last be changed to joy.

* * *

Elizabeth's sharp memory also delighted in recalling her friendship with Elizabeth Sadler. She could still see Sad's every feature and expression, and could bring to her mind's eye every article of furniture and each plant surrounding Sad in her home.

Lively as the nor'westers, Elizabeth's children, too, could tell every article of Sad's room upstairs: where the sofa stood on which Sad sat, the little bird, the wooden cow, the white dog. That day, Mother Seton and children had just been dining round the old breakfast table on roast pork and stewed apples like true Yankees. As they reminisced together, all those around the circle gave a sigh, and then concluded with a silent kiss for their mother.

If Eliza Sadler could come to Saint Joseph's, Elizabeth Seton would be truly proud to present her "treasures" to her again: *my* Anna, *my* William, *my* Richard, *my* Kate, *my* Rebecca, she wrote her. If only Eliza could see Rebecca on her knees milking her little white cow, and afterwards striding along with a little tin pail in each hand, the milk running over, and her eyes glistening with delight at the wonders she could do. Kate's greatest pleasure was feeding the lambs with salt from her hand; Ann's was decking the graves of her dear aunts, Cecilia and Harriet Seton. Chiefly, Elizabeth wanted Sad to come and hear the interesting history which had followed Anna's inexperienced and childish romance with Charles du Pavillon of Martinique.

As for William and Richard, they seemed to find great pleasure in asking their mother unceasing questions about all her friends and connections in New York, and about their hopes and prospects in life. Elizabeth wrote her:

> You would have laughed some days ago, as I did, to hear William explaining to Rebecca and Kitty that Aunt and Uncle Sadler, he remembered well, were only dearest friends of mother and papa, but Aunt Sadler was not my own sister like Aunt Post.[8]

Regretfully, Elizabeth told Sad she was obliged to give a half assent to William's earnest statement.

While undergoing the hardships of the first winter in the Stone House and waiting to move into the White House (their new home, then under construction), Elizabeth Seton had written Eliza Sadler: "Come next May to look at our mountains. You will find my plants in lovely order."[9] Referring to herself and her children, she had continued: "The parent root to be sure is almost sapless and appears quite decayed, but when the wind blows hard the little ones surround and bear it up."[10] How Elizabeth wished that Sad could breathe their mountain air and enjoy the repose of their Valley's deep woods and streams.

One May evening, Elizabeth's heart felt as bright as the sun then setting and wished that she could pass the hour of sunset with Sad. "Yet, dearest Eliza, let it be so in spirit."[11] As the summer passed, Elizabeth wrote again:

It is certain that this so much wished favor is in the power of Him who grants me so many favors and I ask it from Him with confidence: that you will with Dué come to the mountain and see your poor friend before she is called — not that I believe the time so short.[12]

Undaunted by their inability to visit with her then, Elizabeth wrote Eliza the following spring that if she had worlds, she would give them to show Sister Dué and Sad the beauty of the mountain's shades in the setting sun, the waving of the wheat fields, the woods covered with flowers and the quiet contented look of their home and its inhabitants. "Say, at least, you will try to come. What is the atom of distance in this world! I tell you *come*, dear Eliza," she wrote her.[13] Elizabeth felt that both Sad and Dué might gain health and amusement by the jaunt as both of them knew on occasion how to forego the "Lady privileges."

But by fall, Elizabeth lamented that neither of them had yet seen the mountain overlooking Saint Joseph's Valley, nor heard the recreation bell, nor had seen the merry children running out of school, nor mounted the old country horses to trot away the rheumatism. This Elizabeth and Anna had tried with great success.

In the summer of 1812, after Anna's death, Elizabeth learned that Eliza Sadler had planned a trip to Wilmington, Delaware, and that if she got to Baltimore, she would come to Saint Joseph's for a visit. Elizabeth informed Sad that on the assumption that Sad had really determined to see her, she had immediately written her friend, Mrs. Chatard, the wife of Dr. Chatard on Saratoga Street in Baltimore. The latter "is the kindest friend I ever found since I left you, and would receive you with every attention."[14] There, Sad would receive every assistance on how to reach Elizabeth.

Elizabeth felt, however, that since there was no "public carriage" from Baltimore to Emmitsburg, it would be next to impossible unless like Mary Post (Elizabeth Seton's sister), Sad had someone to drive her in the stagecoach. "There is only a stage hack of $25 charge from there here — and how could I ask it, my Eliza."[15] At the end of the summer, Elizabeth again wrote Sad:

> My Eliza, a traveller so far and so far, and returned home without seeing the lovely mountains. There is a mixture of many feelings in the reflection — so many difficulties in getting here, and from what Sister [Post] said of the roads even dangers — but to have seen my Eliza, placed my dear ones in her arms, carried her to the little sacred wood of rest and repose, introducing her to some of my smiling companions — but after *that*, the long long sigh of separation. So He provides, dear Eliza.[16]

The next summer, news reached Elizabeth Seton that Catherine Dupleix (Dué), who had recently become a Catholic, might visit Saint Joseph's. The very idea was extravagant. What a delight it would be: the possibility of seeing Dué was like a foretaste of heaven. If she was delayed only by the fear of not finding entrance at Saint Joseph's House, Elizabeth wanted Sad to tell her that:

> the front door, the back, the side door which will lead her in the chapel and all the windows up and down will open at her approach with her maid, who I would rather she should leave behind, if she does not want her as a companion. We will make all go right, if once we meet.[17]

On Saratoga Street in Baltimore, opposite Saint John's Church close by Bishop Carroll's, Mrs. Chatard would receive Dué "as an accomplished pious French woman treats the friend of her dearest friend." Dué would find there Elizabeth's bed in which "our dear little lame Rebecca had been nursed two months." If the pillows were silk and the quilt was of down, Dué must do penance in advance for the hard ones she would find at Saint Joseph's. From then on, every noise, every bark of the dog made a "look out" for Dué.

About Dué's conversion, Elizabeth wrote Sad: "And my Dué dear is really so courageous as to hold up her head to the world in a case where her poor friend [Elizabeth Seton] looked and often felt like a culprit — but so it is."[18]

A subsequent letter to Sad read:

> You shall know at least this happy Tuesday night 28th,
> Dué is safe and surrounded with love and tenderness;
> some pain, no doubt but she says she is in perfect health
> compared to the beginning of the journey. Could you see
> my heart in the silence of this moment while she rests!
> Peace, peace, my Eliza![19]

Elizabeth later wrote Antonio Filicchi, her friend in Leghorn, Italy: "Mrs Dupleix, too, through storms and difficulties (to which mine were but gentle breezes) is safe also in the ark of refuge" (the Catholic Church).[20]

Ostensibly, the mountains facing Saint Joseph's Valley seemed the limits of Elizabeth's world, but beyond them, Elizabeth had "many most dear interests." Not the least of them was Sad's eternal happiness. This thought came into Elizabeth's mind "a thousand times more often than many others." Since Elizabeth's occupations were congenial with Sad's mind, Elizabeth felt that, perhaps, of all who ever knew her, Sad was the only one who could justly appreciate Elizabeth's means of happiness. Some years ago in New York with both on their knees, Sad had promised Elizabeth to look to Almighty God alone for strength and love in her every trial and suffering. But since that precious moment, Sad had allowed doubts to come into her heart. How there could really exist persons who doubt a future life puzzled Elizabeth; possessing affections and tenderness of heart, they must feel the necessity of a place of reunion. Elizabeth's loving heart could find no words sufficient to express her love for Sad — a love she sought.

To clear away Sad's doubt of a future life, Elizabeth wanted her to again see Bishop Cheverus of Boston. Elizabeth herself had done this during her doubts about the teachings of the Church. If Sad should have the happiness to hear Bishop Cheverus preach, she would participate in the consolation that Elizabeth had greatly wished her to enjoy. "Yet everybody has different colored eyes and different ears on such occasions and perhaps ours may not agree, but I believe they will," she wrote her.[21] She recalled for Sad how often they had looked at Bishop Cheverus' purple ring and kissed it, and how he had carried Elizabeth and her children in his heart. The children loved him with a sentiment not easily described but which Sad might well imagine. He was also the *cher confrère* of their beloved friend, the Reverend Tisserant, "who had the advantage of Bishop Cheverus exteriorly but not in the spirit of the mind."

Elizabeth knew well that Sad had the secret of integrating all her decisions and works with the dispensations of God. She wrote her:

> So long you have reposed yourself in the arms of your heavenly Father and drawn the sweetest consolations from the love of your Savior, and now that you are called upon to exert that love and confidence will you be alarmed, and seek for human support from so frail a creature as your poor Sister.[22]

Elizabeth wanted Sad to be faithful to God with her whole heart and never *fear*. "The greatest sin you can commit is to fear He will forsake your dear soul when it is struggling to be His," she admonished.[23] In the Eucharist, Sad would find "instant peace and balm to every wound." If Sad would meet Him there, at least in spirit, and make it her unceasing request to receive Him with true faith in Holy Communion, then there, she and Elizabeth could mix their prayers and tears together.

One morning, when Elizabeth presented Sad to Jesus again in the midst of her "tenderest love and most earnest desires, He seemed to say: 'Peace, poor heart, your prayer is heard; she is mine and in my own good time I will seal her so.'"[24] The blessing which Sad was seeking was God's gift alone. "Only let me repeat to you," wrote Elizabeth, "leave all in Him."

For several years, during the serious illness of Elizabeth Seton's youngest daughter, Rebecca, much of Elizabeth's writing was curtailed. But, when Sad's letter arrived after Rebecca's death, Elizabeth's cheek began to burn the moment she saw her handwriting. Then, after reading the letter, Elizabeth's heart began to shake at Sad's first impression of Elizabeth's long silence: It was so far from the true cause of the silence. Elizabeth's answer read thus:

Far from religion being a source of coldness or neglect towards you, that it is that very identical point in your and my little compass of life that brings my thoughts and often liveliest imaginations closest to you, not as you might suppose, ever dear friend, as it relates to our views of Faith (for that most delicate and sacred subject I have long since learned to leave to God except where my duty is explicit), but as it relates to our taste and habits of life — mine being exactly what you would most fondly delight in, that over and over, I have said and most frequently now say to myself, if only dear Sad could see it and know it — for your *Matron step* and *quiet look* and independent *intention* are now precisely the rule of my life.[25]

Elizabeth wanted Sad to trust her sincerity and to spare her the repeated allegation that now Sad was less dear to her. "When all hearts are made known, you will know how dearly, my Eliza [Sad], *I love you*, and how much I would do to prove that love," she concluded.[26] Instead of long attention in prayer, Elizabeth counselled Sad to try to keep her heart with God and to speak its pains to Him with that reliance on His love and mercy that she had so long experienced. "Not one sigh or pang is unnoticed by Him."[27]

At the death of her husband, the resigned and comforted Sad took herself off to France. When the first echo of "Mrs. Sadler gone to Paris" had reached the mountains, Elizabeth and her daughter, Kate, answered it with so many oh's and ah's that it would have amused Eliza to hear them. Obliged to stop there in ignorance of what could have made Sad do precisely what she and Kate so often would have liked to have done, Elizabeth wrote Sad:

Do let me enjoy my pleasure and the playful laugh of my heart to think you have done so drole [*sic*] a thing. I think I should have been a traveller, too, if I had had no burdens to nail me.[28]

With the passing of time, however, Elizabeth's health was noticeably failing. In her few remaining years, Elizabeth continued to pray for Sad and Dué. They were remembered at Mass "where it is the greatest blessing to be remembered." She sent them a thousand loves and benedictions and a special love to all she loved in New York. Her faithful affection for them would go with her to the grave.

CHAPTER 10

SIMON GABRIEL BRUTÉ
My Priest Friend And My Final Strength

Elizabeth Ann Seton and the Reverend Simon Gabriel Bruté first met in Emmitsburg, Maryland, in the summer of 1811.[1] Fr. Bruté, a member of the Society of Saint Sulpitius, had sailed from France as a missionary and as part of a group returning to Baltimore with the rules of the Daughters of Charity of Saint Vincent de Paul. These rules were to serve as a model for Elizabeth Seton's infant community of Sisters of Charity of Saint Joseph's — named such since Elizabeth Seton had called the site of their first foundation Saint Joseph's Valley.

In Baltimore, Fr. Bruté was named a director of Saint Mary's Seminary and appointed to teach a class of philosophy in the adjoining college. At the end of the school year, however, he was sent to assist the Rev. John DuBois, founder of Mount Saint Mary's College in Emmitsburg, who had recently been appointed spiritual director of Elizabeth Seton's sisterhood. Both priests became involved in the work of adapting the French rules to meet the needs of the

American community. On August 9, 1811, Elizabeth Seton wrote about Fr. Bruté to Archbishop John Carroll:

> Fr. Bruté in the purity of his heart is doing his very best, and much more than it could possibly be supposed so young a man would venture on, to second all the plans lately adopted.[2]

Although Fr. Bruté's sojourn in Emmitsburg that summer was brief, a deep and lasting friendship began between him and Elizabeth Seton.

In Fr. Bruté, Elizabeth Seton had found a kindred spirit. He so impressed her, her children and the community, that by Christmas Elizabeth wrote to the Rev. Pierre Babade who had befriended them on their arrival in Baltimore: "He so reminds us all of you that we who call you Father, call him Brother among ourselves."[3]

Like Fr. Babade, Fr. Bruté had taken a vital interest not only in Elizabeth's community, but also in her children. At his return to Saint Mary's Seminary in Baltimore in the fall, he kept informed on the affairs at Saint Joseph's Valley and tried to lighten Elizabeth's heavy burden. When Annina, Elizabeth's oldest daughter, then seventeen years old, was very ill and lay dying, Fr. Bruté was happy to learn that she had written her *Act of Consecration* to God and that she had been received as a novice in the Sisters of Charity. Then when it was believed that she was at the point of death, Fr. Bruté managed to go to Emmitsburg to be at her bedside and administer the Sacrament of Healing. At the sight of him, Annina joyfully presented her hands to him for anointing. At her death, Fr. Bruté appealed to Elizabeth in tears and deep sorrow to keep her thoughts focused on eternity and on the joy of seeing God face-to-face. He felt Annina was in heaven. "What thinks she of the little nothing of our

Earth," he asked. He wanted Elizabeth to think of her present duties as a gift to her Redeemer. He wrote her:

> O Mother, how much good [there is] to do in your blessed family; what a celestial commission intrusted to you, mother of daughters of charity to whom also so much is [given] to do for God and souls through this short life.[4]

He taught her again to see the graveyard as a "delightful little wood, happy little corner of the world."[5]

In the summer following Annina's death, Fr. Bruté (already known as the "Seraphim") was engaged in missionary work at two missions on the eastern shore of Maryland. Speaking only broken English, he felt inadequate to his missionary work for souls. In discouragement at the failures due to his awkward English, he wrote to Elizabeth Seton in French:

> I spoke again to a congregation so rough, so sad, so boisterous that you would have suffered, mother of charity, to have heard me. I no longer know in these two fleeting visits how to take a tone simple, sweet, tranquil and instructive, which alone, I feel will produce solid fruits.[6]

Fr. Bruté had appealed again and again for Elizabeth's assistance. To give expression to her own zeal for souls, Elizabeth, quite fluent in French, helped him not only to develop his homilies and his class lectures but also to deliver them in acceptable English. Meanwhile, she also put into English for him passages of letters received from France. These he gave to his priest-friends, Bishop Flaget, Fr. David and Fr. DuBourg "who could do so much good" with them. In gratitude, Fr. Bruté later wrote Elizabeth:

> You whom I like to call a mother here [she was 4½ years older than Bruté] as I call one in France . . . You have so well helped me better to know, yes better still, a priest of his as I was, to know my happiness and desire, but also [I] so vainly desire to impart the same to others to know and love and say Jesus . . .[7]

This dependence on each other served to strengthen their friendship.

Nothing could have afforded Fr. Bruté greater pleasure than the cheering news he received later that summer from Rev. John M. Tessier, his superior in Baltimore. On September 28, 1812, he was to go to Emmitsburg to assist the Rev. John DuBois at Mount Saint Mary's College and to act as spiritual director for Elizabeth and her community. He wrote happily to a friend:

> My prospect is, as soon as returned to Baltimore [from his missionary endeavors] to go and live with Fr. DuBois at Mount Saint Mary's. I have already received my mission for that purpose.[8]

Delightedly, he celebrated Mass for the Sisters Monday, Tuesday, Wednesday and Thursday.

Shortly after he had assumed his post in Emmitsburg, one of Fr. Bruté's first functions in behalf of Elizabeth's community was to give the homily at the funeral of Sr. Maria (Murphy) Burke who died unexpectedly on October 15, 1812. When Sr. Ellen Thompson died in November of the next year, Fr. Bruté exclaimed to Elizabeth Seton:

> O happy Mother! Already three of your daughters are in Heaven, without counting the two first ones,* those affectionate sisters whom your example has also conducted there. Give, give thanks and redouble your zeal to follow these celestial souls.[9]

In approaching the "little wood," Fr. Bruté was absorbed with the thought of an eternity filled with praise and love.

Charged with directing Elizabeth, Fr. Bruté felt deeply his responsibility toward her. More than anyone else, he seemed to know the secret of her inner strength. From the very beginning, his advice to her was: "Make all happy, open-hearted, supernaturally minded about you." Questioning himself, he asked:

> What am I doing to help you sanctify yourself with a purity and fervor always increasing? But what can I do? What better than [recommend] *simplicity, peace, abandon, daily fidelity, upright intentions, all* and entirely each one of them directed to God *alone*, in our Lord.[10]

As librarian at Mount Saint Mary's from 1812-1814, Fr. Bruté frequently recommended the life of St. Francis of Assisi. "It is the very suavity and unction of Saint Francis de Sales with something of a higher heaven," he wrote her.[11]

Elizabeth Seton loved the priesthood as a divine and glorious service, and saw in Fr. Bruté another Christ, "a visible savior." When she heard priests preach the word of God in a manner unworthy of so important a sacred function, she was pained. Writing to a friend about Elizabeth on this matter, Fr. Bruté, realizing his own failings, exclaimed:

---

* Harriet and Cecilia Seton, Elizabeth's sisters-in-law.

O, that priests felt for themselves as Mother Seton felt they ought to be! How much did she not suffer in witnessing their imperfections! How sorrowfully, yet charitably did she consider their faults.[12]

Elizabeth herself had a great fear of offending God and begged Fr. Bruté "in the name of our Eternity" to tell her everything she might do to prove her love for Him. She felt consoled that God recognized in her heart the thirst to see Him better served and loved.

Elizabeth opened her heart freely to Fr. Bruté, whom she fondly called *G*. He had led her to the deep realization of the immensity of God, of His presence in the world. He encouraged her to adore Him in the Blessed Sacrament and to "skip up to the scene where all will be revealed," namely, that Jesus is one with God and yet dwells in Elizabeth's heart, that *G* was also in the "bosom of her Jesus who does all in him as He does in my poor daily part." This same Jesus is in the Tabernacles and on our altar. Ever faithful, He is in the graces of the moment, in the desolations of her heart, in the aridity of her prayers as she kneels beneath the crucifix, and in her very sorrow for sins. *G*'s chalice alone, she felt, could adequately thank God. Fr. Bruté wrote her:

> You understand, my mother, only with such an increase of peace and amiableness to all around you, trying so gently to gain every heart to so good a God [can you succeed]. But, indeed, if I preach [to] you, it is to preach [to] me the [one who is] most distant from that happy point of duty.[13]

Entreating Elizabeth to help him with her advice and to use the utmost freedom in her remarks, he exclaimed:

O! if my true love is not yet worthy enough of all yours, and your trust, do try me again, and see how willing I will be to mend everything in order to assist you all.[14]

In November 1814 when Fr. Bruté learned of his unexpected appointment as president of Saint Mary's College in Baltimore, he made ready a voyage to France. Presumably among other reasons lurking in his heart, he had an ardent desire to see his mother, to acquire his own library and to recruit missioners for the Church in America. This event coincided with the birthday of Elizabeth Seton's oldest son, William, who had just turned eighteen. Eager for William to be associated with Antonio and Filippo Filicchi in their counting house in Leghorn, Italy, and encouraged by Fr. DuBois, Elizabeth arranged for William to be accompanied by Fr. Bruté to Europe. Indeed, if time allowed, Fr. Bruté intended to go with him to Leghorn. For William to be travelling with Fr. Bruté, Elizabeth felt as "secure as good old Tobias felt." Together, they sailed on the *Tontine* on April 6, 1815, and docked at Bordeaux, France about six weeks later.

In a letter of introduction to Antonio Filicchi, Elizabeth wrote him:

My dear Sir, — This letter will introduce to you the Rev. Fr. Bruté, a most distinguished soul, as you will know in a moment if you have ever the happiness of a personal acquaintance.

There is no possible recommendation I could give him which would not be ratified by our Most. Rev. Archbishop and the blessed Cheverus, by whom he is most highly beloved and esteemed. Our Archbishop, indeed, values him as an inestimable treasure in the Church, and you will find, if you have the happiness to know him yourself that his uncommon piety, learning and excellent qualifications (and even his family, since you Europeans take that into account), entitle him to the distinguished friendship and regard of Filippo and of yourself. He has adopted the great interest of my William so generously that with yourselves, I consider him our truest friend in God. What more can your little sister say to interest you? Judge for yourself.[15]

Away from Emmitsburg, Fr. Bruté tried to fulfill his sacred trust to Elizabeth. Arriving at Bordeaux and finding unforeseen changes which would hasten his return to Baltimore, he wrote the Filicchis on May 24, 1815 that it was impossible for him to accompany William Seton to Leghorn as he had intended. He told them that he had seen William off for Marseilles with a passport and letter from the American consul in Bordeaux to the one in Leghorn. He added:

> I love him very dearly, and hope that he will be happy where he is going, and will give you all the satisfaction which your kindness to his excellent mother calls for. This incomparable woman, whose views are of the most elevated order, sends you letters by her son.[16]

Enclosing his Bordeaux address, Fr. Bruté told the Filicchis he expected to remain in France until the end of July and hoped to have a letter from them to present to Elizabeth Seton.

When he received William's letter, Fr. Bruté was pleased to learn that his friend, Mr. Preudhomme de Borre, had helped William to arrive safely in Leghorn about the middle of July. While in Marseilles, William was received into the house of Madame de Saint-Césaire, the sister of

Mr. Preudhomme. She was pleased to call him her son, and they parted in tears. Likewise, he was cordially received by the Filicchis.

After the white flag was raised indicating the end of the Napoleonic Wars, Fr. Bruté made his way north to his home in Rennes to see his mother. In a letter to William dated July 17, 1815, Fr. Bruté told him that he had written Mr. Preudhomme to thank him for his attentions to him. He continued:

> Give my respects to your friends, and say how pleased I would feel could I for a moment be with them to join you in speaking of such a worthy friend of theirs as your mother is, a friend for heaven and eternity, and whose constant delight is to recall all that they have done for her in that direction.[17]

He admitted to William that he felt very miserable for not being able to fulfill towards him more satisfactorily his mother's wishes. He asked William to love him in return for his love. Before enclosing his Paris address, he wrote: "Let us pray one for the other."

Then Fr. Bruté sailed on the *Blooming Rose* on October 17, 1815 from Bordeaux for Baltimore. While on shipboard he again wrote William Seton asking him to pray for his safe arrival in America that he might speak to "Mother Seton" about him, and give her his letters and those the Filicchis had entrusted to him.

When Fr. Bruté arrived in Baltimore on November 28, 1815, one of his three companions, a young Irish student, entered the Baltimore Seminary. Fr. Bruté's appointment as president of Saint Mary's Seminary was officially confirmed by his superior, the Reverend John M. Tessier, who noted it in his *Journal* on December 18, 1815.

At his return to Emmitsburg, Elizabeth wrote Fr. Bruté:

> You would never believe, dear G, the good *your return* does to this soul of your little mother — to see you *again* tearing yourself from all that is dearest — giving up again the full liberty you lawfully and justly possessed — exchanging for a truly heavy chain, and the endless labyrinth of discussions and wearisome details to give the softest expressions.[18]

When he was to leave so soon again to assume his new position at Saint Mary's in Baltimore, Elizabeth confessed tearfully:

> A volume would not have been enough to say half the heart [contained], that [heart which] fastens to yours more and more, if possible, but with such freedom of the local circumstances or position of the moment, that I shall see you go again to fulfill your Presidentship (O bad omen, G.) I did not know that tear was there.[19]

Nor was Elizabeth alone in missing Fr. Bruté. She repeated to him what Fr. Charles Duhamel, pastor at Saint Joseph's Church in Emmitsburg, had said to her about him:

> They tell me to my face now that Fr. Bruté's gone, all is gone. Some say they will not go to confession till he comes again. Poor dear good Bruté, did you see his letter, ma'm to everybody, to save souls? — He could tend six

congregations at least. He can do what would kill ten men, if you only give him bread and two or three horses to ride to death, one after t'other.[20]

Fr. Bruté, "this authoritative exhorter," had also won the hearts of Elizabeth's children and the Sisters, and had endeared himself to the Archbishop. If Fr. Bruté could hear the comments, Elizabeth noted, he would laugh heartily. "I hear nothing else." Rebecca, her youngest daughter, exclaimed, "How I do love him." And Kitty, Elizabeth's next to the youngest, said that day, "Mother, if I had no other reason to be good but just to get to heaven and be always with the 'Brother', I would try with all my might." With ready tears, Elizabeth then urged them all "to pray much for him [Fr. Bruté] to our God." When Mrs. Haws said, in full simplicity, "I do not think I ever saw a saint upon earth but Mr. Bruté — dear Mr. Bruté," Elizabeth wrote him: "Let them think so for Our Lord's sake."[21] The "good Archbishop," too, had commented how unfortunate it was that Fr. Bruté was going. "Will he ever return?" he added, "I hope so, indeed, and that very soon."[22] Elizabeth feared for Fr. Bruté that he was too much loved by all and wrote him that she would rather he should be in China than too much a "darling" here, adding, "It is only because they do not know you, my son — yet those who know you so well, do they love less?"[23]

Elizabeth wanted Fr. Bruté to do well the hard work before him, and took it as her most serious duty to pray for him and get prayers from all those "most innocent hearts." For his full fidelity, she said, she would try always to bring him the support of a "Mother's prayer." One day, she was truly downhearted at his absence, yet she said incessantly, "Glory to the Father, Son and Holy Spirit, with its 100 meanings." She encouraged Fr. Bruté to look up confidently. Jesus would not leave him in weakness who had left all for His sake. "No, no, no *G*. He will *not*," she repeated.[24]

Elizabeth Seton prayed often for Fr. Bruté's success in his spiritual endeavors as president of Saint Mary's Seminary. At times, when he was prone to excess, Elizabeth cautioned him in his "restless desires to gain a heart or unfold a temper." When a group of thirteen missionaries of the Congregation of the Mission led by the Rev. Felix de Andreis visited Fr. Bruté in the summer of 1816, Elizabeth, filled with joy, directed the Sisters to offer their communions in thanksgiving for "the blessed Missioners sent to enlighten our savage land."[25] Later, she urged Fr. Bruté to pity and pray incessantly for the "poor blind [souls] lost to love and duty, groping along through the bright heavenly light which shines so lovely to the happy ones who *comprehend*."[26] "Can you lift your chalice without thinking of them?" she asked him.[27]

A missionary at heart, Elizabeth asked Fr. Bruté to pray as much for her as she for him, and later commented: "The same fidelity in all the rest and I would be as you bid me a *Saint*."[28] She avowed to him that while she kept the right distance from him in her exterior actions, yet, in her heart, that was "quite another thing." In proportion as her pride in him increased, she felt keenly her own littleness and her seemingly empty sacrifice to God. She wrote him: "I am ambitious (indeed *G* often with many tears) to get up with you a little by a generous will, and more faithful service in the little I can do."[29]

Although Elizabeth Ann Seton and Simon Gabriel Bruté were separated for two years, their bond of friendship never slackened. Still bent on sharing Elizabeth's burden, Fr. Bruté continued his correspondence with her son, William, in Leghorn, and interceded in obtaining a position in Baltimore for Richard, her second son, who had just graduated from Mount Saint Mary's College and had come of age to earn his own living. But it was on Rebecca (fourteen years old) that Fr. Bruté showered his affection and wrote the "dear sufferer" consoling letters in return for her notes to him. Four years earlier while Annina was very ill, Rebecca had slipped on some ice and injured her leg. At the time, she tried to keep the pain to herself, but as time went on (despite the attention of Dr. Wright Post, her New York uncle, and some of the best doctors in Baltimore and Philadelphia) the mishap left Rebecca lame. Impressed by Bec's faith throughout her suffering, Fr. Bruté wrote her:

> Rebecca, my Sister — I thank you for your little note. I have pasted it in the last page of my Bible, the one that your mother gave me. I am just from the altar.... At the communion, I took you in my heart and offered you to our Lord as completely as I could.[30]

The next time he wrote her in large letters the names Jesus, Mary, Joseph and then added:

> It is your Father, your God of love and salvation ... my dear Bec, not I, in any of these little black writing spots; He, not the flower you admire — the little food which feeds your spark of life — ah, more, He even in what only still truly pleases you and makes you so happy in your pains and fainting — your *mother*. He himself mostly seen in her smile, her maternal voice, her quickening and animated look. He in all, my Rebecca; and let the storms roar around the walls and the grates of this transitory hard lazaretto of life; let sufferings, cruel and unrelenting, bid you stand and watch when the smallest bird enjoys his rest, let, let, let — the soul still knows how to cheer up, seeing

and feeling her God, her Father, and Almighty lover in all.... One look to your bleeding Jesus will restore more strength and resolution than the most wearisome night would have taken away.[31]

Your Brother

Rebecca's love for Fr. Bruté was as bountiful as his love for her. When Elizabeth wanted to put away his picture, Rebecca insisted, "No, no, nowhere but opposite my eyes at the foot of my bed."[32] As fall approached, it became obvious that Rebecca's health was rapidly declining. About the middle of October, when Elizabeth feared that "sweet Bec must go," Fr. Bruté hastened to Emmitsburg. He was accompanied by Dr. Pierre Chatard, the Sisters' physician in Baltimore, who confirmed Elizabeth's fear. Rebecca's joy and gratitude at seeing Fr. Bruté were not even slightly dimmed at the Doctor's pronouncement. Fr. Bruté had come to be at her bedside until her last moment. His presence seemed a security to her against all the power of the enemy. Keeping up her cheerful smiles, she begged him to say his office near her. Though seeing only his back, she would express to Elizabeth by signs and looks at the crucifix her peace and contentment. She liked to recall how Fr. Bruté used to call their little room "the Tabernacle of the Just." Several days before Rebecca died, Fr. Bruté heard her confession and gave her a blessing. On All Saints' Day, he brought her Holy Viaticum. Two days later, the last moment had come. Rebecca, still alert, dropped her head for the last time on Elizabeth's breast. Fr. Bruté wrote his sympathy to William, who was still in Leghorn.

After Rebecca's death, Elizabeth expressed her gratitude for Fr. Bruté's loving interest:

Well, at least, my blessed Father, you are acquitted and all that the kindest best invention of the most compassionate heart could do has been done by you, to carry me thro' this hard moment which is past and gone as easily as if our high comforter had spread his soft wings over every fiber.[33]

The following year, 1817, while Fr. Bruté occupied the president's chair and suite at Saint Mary's Seminary, it was obvious that his heart was sighing for the mountain of Emmitsburg. Besides, he had left a void that no one else could fill. Elizabeth, too, wished for his return, but she was bent on his doing God's will to its "most full and complete accomplishment." His responsibilities were of an eternal consequence. Earlier she had written him: "You did not leave *all*, the whole delight of your France and family, but to do His only will."[34] He knew the only security and heavenly peace rested on this essential *abandon* to God's will, "so at least you taught me," she said. She promised to take God by storm with prayers until they would know the *final* word on his return. She wanted him to read well her whole heart in this *resignation*. On the feast of the Holy Trinity in June, she wrote him:

Will you please to bless the happiest of women in the Holy Trinity on this day (always excepting those who love better) and be your dear Reverence blessed.[35]

Toward the end of the year, Fr. Bruté was sent temporarily to Emmitsburg to replace Fr. Duhamel who had been very ill and was near death, and to assist Fr. DuBois over the holidays. At Fr. Duhamel's death, Fr. Tessier, realizing Fr. DuBois' absolute need of Fr. Bruté, appointed him to the mountain in February 1818. Fr. Bruté wrote Elizabeth:

> In this new beginning, it seems as [if] we all together [should] want to renew our best confidence in Our Lord Himself, for how can I hope to be His blessed instrument but through His adorable will, and most tender mercies to souls so entirely offered to Him in the ways of His most perfect service on earth. Indeed, let all be confidence, all pure faith and love and we may be sure His grace will be confirmed in every heart, even by the most unworthy and unfit instrument.[36]

Elizabeth was elated at Fr. Bruté's return. She answered him:

> As to confidence, Devoted Love, and happy heart our dear Savior *is my witness* that no soul could be more blessed than mine with regard to you — too much for the few days of my life.[37]

Instead of the war of nature which was so long her daily health battle, she now reflected with God in secret on her present willingness *to live* (so different from the past *nine years dragging*). She found her tranquil dispositions a continual feast. She was "so in love then with rules that she saw the *bit* of the bridle all gold, and the *reins* all of silk."[38] If Fr. Bruté could feel as she did, that the union of Sisters Betsey, Joanna and Margaret with her in the management of Saint Joseph's Valley was due to his presence there, he would bless God as she did in *Peace*.[39]

In the remaining few years of Elizabeth's life, she and Fr. Bruté continued to see each other, although mainly in the confessional because of his spiritual direction of the Sisters and their growing community. Then, on a Sunday morning, September 20, 1820, Elizabeth's failing health had taken a serious turn. Thinking Elizabeth was near death, two Sisters hastened to the nearby Saint Joseph's parish to notify Fr. Bruté of this sudden change. He immediately mounted his horse, galloped down the rough road to the White House and prepared to administer Extreme Unction to Elizabeth. Still conscious and alert, Elizabeth confessed her sins aloud to him. Afterwards, the Sisters gathered around Elizabeth and together with Fr. Bruté prayed the Our Father and *Confiteor* to gain the indulgence of the sacrament.

That day, Fr. Bruté visited Elizabeth several times to see if she wanted or needed anything. After Benediction when he again went to her room, Elizabeth consented with all her heart to the request that he ask for prayers from her friends. The next morning before 5 o'clock, Fr. Bruté was again at her bedside in prayer. As he prepared for Mass, he suggested to her that she make a spiritual communion, since she had not been able to fast from midnight. Regretting this, he wanted her to keep united with the Lord: "His love, His will, His peace." Elizabeth appeared eager to do this. Several days later on the feast of the Rosary, October 1, 1820, Fr. Bruté brought Elizabeth Holy Viaticum. Then, on the feast days that followed, he brought her Holy Communion. Each time after Communion, a great peace came over her.

During the months that Elizabeth rallied and seemed to be improving, Fr. Bruté's visits were less frequent, but his interest had not lessened. When he visited Elizabeth on New Year's Day 1821, he found that her condition had worsened, and gave her absolution. Then, two days before her death on January 4, 1821, because she had shown a marked improvement in the interim, she again received Extreme

Unction. The next morning, when Fr. Bruté stepped into her room, Elizabeth was "quiet." That afternoon his last words to her were: "Ask Heaven to praise and love Him."

Despite Fr. Bruté's frequent visits and solicitude during Elizabeth's last agony, he was not present to give her his final blessing before she drew her last breath. She died fifteen minutes before he arrived. In all her suffering, drawing strength from Fr. Bruté's presence and ministering, Elizabeth's greatest consolation was the moments she had spent with Jesus in Holy Communion. Mass was celebrated the following day and her remains were laid to rest in the graveyard of the Sisters of Charity of Saint Joseph's with tears and regrets.[39]

The poetic lines that follow are said to have been written by Fr. Bruté:

> Here let the poor, the orphan, come to mourn;
> Let Mercy weep; for this is Seton's urn.
> Here let religion's sighs and tears be given;
> Ah! no; she smiles again and points to Heaven.[40]

Simon Gabriel Bruté remained in Emmitsburg until October 28, 1834, when he accepted the bishopric created for him in Vincennes, Indiana, where he died on June 28, 1839.

EPILOGUE

The range and number of Elizabeth Ann Seton's friendships indicate a remarkably attractive, adaptive and strong person. Most of us feel fortunate if we have one or two intimate friends who often enough are somewhat like ourselves. But she seemed to resonate with a variety of persons and somehow found the strength to support them all with only minimal neglect.

Consider how diverse were her friendships. Her father, Dr. Richard Bayley, was a sophisticated man with a strong scientific bent. Though a so-called "martyr of charity for the immigrant," he did not appear as a particularly religious person. He doted on his daughter because she could understand his values. Yet he could allow his disciplined life of service to take him away from her for as much as four years and to put his relatives to raising her. Notwithstanding this, father and daughter idolized each other.

Elizabeth's husband William was something of a wealthy *bon vivant*, charming, effervescent, artistic. Though not of sturdy health, he was a dutiful man who later under the stress of suffering and with the tenderness of Elizabeth became a devout Christian. His gallant ways and attentiveness made him quite attractive to the twenty-year-old Elizabeth; his later patience under duress deeply endeared him to her.

Antonio Filicchi, the highly successful international businessman, combined a romantic adventurism with a devout faith. He found the very direct and beautiful Elizabeth almost irresistible as she struggled, quite alone, to take care of her five children and to find the true Church. This man of integrity proved to be a faithful friend, a provider for many of Elizabeth's needs over decades of time and the distances of oceans. Elizabeth never stopped loving him intensely.

When Elizabeth was running the Seton household of eighteen people including her own two small children and the seven children of the recently deceased William Seton, Sr., she found, to her surprise, help and companionship from Rebecca Seton, his eighteen-year-old daughter. The youthful Rebecca became a quiet center of stability alongside Elizabeth. Indeed, Rebecca's smiling generosity was pushed to the breaking point by the heavy duties placed on her by all the relatives. Her remarkably mature qualities of warmth and steadfastness deepened under the constant pressures of helping to run a huge household of children, servants and visiting relatives. She became like a favorite sister of Elizabeth who wanted her always in sight to experience her touch, her glance, her soft voice.

Quite another person was Julia Scott of Philadelphia's and New York's high society, the favorite of Elizabeth's father. She was the lavish entertainer, the worldly lady of nightly concerts and parties. Naturally vain, she was also mercurial, yet full of relaxed affection for people — so much so that Elizabeth felt more at ease with her than with anyone else and poured out everything helter-skelter to her. Underneath all the sophistication was a loyal and generous woman about whose salvation Elizabeth worried.

In startling contrast to Julia was Cecilia Seton, Elizabeth's youngest friend. While still in her teens, she had been put at the head of a family of eight children even though, to her brother's consternation, she had become a Catholic convert at fifteen. As a result, she was compelled to leave her family temporarily — until she was needed to mother her brother's eight children. Her health, too, was precarious; yet she sturdily took on all the tasks and the long hours of entertaining, nursing, disciplining and cuddling the young children. Meanwhile, she and Elizabeth nurtured each other's Catholic faith amid the relatives' hostility and developed an easily shared spirituality which involved not only hard work seven days a week but also long periods of prayer-emptiness together.

Catherine Dupleix (Dué) and Eliza Sadler (Sad) were New York society matrons of strong loyalty to Elizabeth. Dué might not be much for letter writing but she was a favorite of Elizabeth's five children, having nursed Rebecca, the youngest child. Despite the criticism of her society friends, Dué bravely entered the Catholic Church and solidly supported the New York orphanage founded by Elizabeth's fellow nuns. Eliza Sadler, on the other hand, specialized in trying to spoil Elizabeth's children even as she strengthened Elizabeth during the latter's familial persecutions. Though a doubter about the future life, she wanted to believe as Elizabeth did, and so felt deeply any apparent neglect on the part of Elizabeth. Without these two friends, Elizabeth's life would have been excruciatingly difficult.

Fortunately, towards the end of Elizabeth's life when the darkness of ill-health, of multiple deaths within her community, and of her own approaching end was enveloping her, she had the light of Simon Gabriel Bruté's friendship. This French Sulpician priest had been forced into administrative and academic work precisely when his heart was much more in pastoral work among the poor. He was a cultured man (later transporting some 5,000 of his books to

Vincennes, Indiana, when appointed Bishop there). But for all this, he was quite simple in his ways, fascinated by children and most empathetic to the latter's hard-working parents. He would even submit his englished sermons and letters to Elizabeth for rudimentary correction and be aghast at the gaucheries his ignorance of English could produce. But this only the more endeared him to Elizabeth who found him the spiritual director she had always dreamed of having.

The number of these intimate friendships astounds the average person who asks: "Where did she find the time and energy to support so many and varied friends?" This is particularly mysterious when one reflects on her lonely childhood when seemingly only the God of nature, so real for her, companioned her. But the Lord seems to have been a great source of strength for her and the loneliness apparently sensitized her to other's needs so that she was ready for friendships, even hungered for them. Remarkably, economic reverses, deaths of husband and relatives, her own difficult conversion within a hostile environment, the severe labors of educating particularly spoiled children — all seemed to be turned into the wine of friendship rather than into the embittering dregs of life.

All this points to Elizabeth's attractiveness for many people. Not only her students (whom she was unafraid to discipline and then to hug a few moments later) but also their parents, particularly the men like Dr. Chatard, Mr. Weis, Mr. O'Conway, General Richard Harper, Mr. Cooper and Mr. Fox, found her lovable and loving. She did not fit the usual pattern of early nineteenth century womanhood. Her poetic and musical talents, her sharp wit and tart tongue, and her delight in dancing made her fun to be with. But at the same time her practical sense and gentle ways appealed to businessmen and priest-educators. Elizabeth could be easily moved to tears by a child's loneliness or a parent's despair, but she could also be a rock of persistent strength through heavy storms.

Then there was her faith, often humorously expressed, sometimes tortured, but almost always luminous, peace-instilling, and challenging for herself and for her friends. No wonder so many of her friends were pulled against the societal tide into the harbor of the Catholic faith where she met them with warm embrace and reassuring smile. Her unpredictability and uniqueness certainly fit her for the title, American saint.

David J. Hassel, S.J.

APPENDIX

THE PARENTS OF STUDENTS
Become More Than Mere Acquaintances For Elizabeth Ann Seton

Through her letters to her friend, Rev. Pierre Babade, who first befriended her in Baltimore, and to the parents of her first boarders (the O'Conways of Philadelphia, the Foxes of New York, the Harpers, the Chatards and the Weises of Baltimore, to name only a few) we get a glimpse of how large a role friendship played in Elizabeth Seton's educational life. Besides instructing the children in the Catholic faith and teaching them Catholic practices, she, as a guardian, was vitally interested in the general well-being of each child entrusted to her care: their health, dispositions and general behavior at Saint Joseph's. This attention extended to their families, some of whom became her close friends.

When Fr. Bruté left Saint Joseph's to become president of Saint Mary's College in Baltimore, Elizabeth wrote him: "I will tell you in what I know American parents to be most difficult — in hearing the faults of their children."[1]

Parents feel that their children's behavior reflects on them. From her own experience of twenty instances, Elizabeth saw that the faults of the children were not to be immediately corrected by the parents, but rather by good advice and education. To the teacher, the parents would say:

> Yes sir, I know, I perceive, [while] in their hearts, they think the fault not so much. They will soften and excuse to the child what they condemn to us, and our efforts afterwards avail very little. So that [is] a big point.[2]

Instead, Elizabeth would express her gratitude to the parents for their confidence in her and in the Sisters, and for their many benefactions. Only through friendship with the parents could the latter be enlisted to help Elizabeth discipline and educate their children.

Saint Joseph's Valley (as Mr. Cooper had envisioned it and as Elizabeth had hoped) was to have been a nursery only for "our Savior's poor country children." But in God's Providence it soon became the means of educating city girls in the faith, as pious wives and mothers. In addition, it later extended itself to instruct children in the orphan asylums of Philadelphia and New York. Finally, towards the end of Elizabeth's career, the Dutch immigrants and others in the Baltimore area were also welcomed into its warm embrace.

For Elizabeth, Fr. Pierre Babade's cordial spirit breathed all through her educational enterprise. So, when Elizabeth received two newborn infants in her arms, she called them "Petrus" for Fr. Babade, signing them with a cross as soon as they came into the world. Later, when Sarah, a friend of Fr. Babade, first stepped in the door at Saint Joseph's, Elizabeth took her hand, then Annina, Elizabeth's daughter, whispered: "Father [Babade] sent her."

Elizabeth wrote: "I loved her before that. How much more afterwards."[3]

Because of Fr. Babade's spirit of cordial friendship, Elizabeth learned to enjoy her arduous task in Saint Joseph's Valley. In a happy mood, she wrote Julia Scott: "I suppose I must be school dame again."[4] "Besides," she admitted later, "our boarders could never manage without the Old Lady [Elizabeth herself]."[5] Elizabeth, despite her intense desire for orderly education, described herself to Eliza Sadler as "a lazy sleepy soul; give me but quiet and all is given." And surprisingly, quiet there was in the midst of children all day, except in the early part of the morning and the last part of the afternoon. When Fr. DuBois became their superior, he seemed to enhance the orderly quiet, other-centered spirit of Fr. Babade. Elizabeth wrote Mrs. Chatard: "He always more and more endeavored to do everything for their [the Sisters' and students'] advantage and good order." Fr. DuBois' unselfish mentorship helped to set the tone for Elizabeth's school and heart. He typified affectionate attention to others.

Within two years, Elizabeth found herself the Mother of more than fifty children of varying ages. Four were about sixteen years old. Elizabeth wrote Sad that she felt bound first to love, instruct and provide for the happiness of all; secondly to give the example of cheerfulness, peace and resignation; and thirdly to consider them more as proceeding from God and going to Him rather than achieving different shades of merit or demerit. "You would recognize," she said, "that manner of looking upon twenty people in the room with a look of affection and interest, showing an interest for all and a concern in all their concern." Within the next four years, by 1816, her household had augmented to "sixty boarders and more, in addition to the country children, and treble the number of Sisters." The quiet order of her school was appreciated; it was the order of attentive affection.

Consequently, situations that disturbed order and harmony at Saint Joseph's pained Elizabeth and, in the beginning, she referred cases to Bishop Carroll. For example, Mr. H---'s daughter had a bold temper and a strong disposition to talk continually of young men. That compelled Elizabeth to insist to Fr. DuBois that he request her father to come and take the girl home without waiting until she made her First Communion, for she was a great hindrance to the rest. Elizabeth felt that the girl was so giddy and unthinking that it would be hard to discover anything about her so that she could be helped to grow into a full womanhood capable of loving sacrifice.

In a second instance, Mr. Coals wrote Sr. Rose about a Miss Nelson who wished to join her student-sister at Saint Joseph's, but without becoming a Sister or being a boarder. This would be an exception to the usual order of admission. So, when Elizabeth learned from the girl's sister (who was much beloved at Saint Joseph's) that the girl had an amiable disposition, and that she was one of Bishop Carroll's favorite children, Elizabeth laid down some stipulations for Bishop Carroll: until the future arrangements at Saint Joseph's were more settled (the matter of the religious constitution for the Sisters and its approval) or until Bishop Carroll could see the Rev. Fr. DuBois, she felt that it would be best, perhaps, to suspend the consideration of Miss Nelson's admission.

It was a quite different case when several years later a long affectionate letter from a Becky Nicholson informed Elizabeth that she was going to consult Bishop Carroll on coming to Saint Joseph's, or when Ellen Wiseman proved to be a pattern of what they would wish all to be at Saint

Joseph's. In this case, the order of attentive affection was enhanced, not disrupted.

Some of the hazards of running a pioneer boarding school would endanger such order. For example, one day Elizabeth King arrived at Saint Joseph's without bed or bedding and with very few articles of clothing. Later, her sisters wrote to deplore her expenses and to inform Elizabeth Seton that upon receipt of their letter, Miss King must not remain at Saint Joseph's one more day as a boarder, but that, if it so pleased her, she could become a Sister.

In response, Elizabeth requested of Miss King's guardian that he send for her and provide for her return journey home, since they had no means of transporting her from Saint Joseph's and the public stagecoach was no nearer than Gettysburg (eight miles away) "even if they could wish a female of her age to go alone in it."[7] As for Miss King's expenses, they were only such as other children had incurred who had arrived under the same circumstances. Further, the gentleman who had brought Miss King to Saint Joseph's suggested no restrictions, and had even directed the Sisters to supply her with whatever she might want.

As for her becoming a Sister, Elizabeth replied: "There are many more requisites than may be imagined by those who do not consider the subject in its sacred point of view."[8] Besides, Miss King had no disposition to be a Sister, nor had she the advantage of a constitution which would recommend her as a useful member for the laborious part of the Sisters' duties. Neither did she possess the mental capacity suited to the object of their institution. For Elizabeth, stark honesty was the basis for good education and possible resultant friendship.

Such cases did not discourage Elizabeth's interest in her students. Caroline Tilghman, after a considerable time at

Saint Joseph's, appeared anxious to receive the sacrament of Baptism. Elizabeth wrote to remind her mother that when Caroline was accepted, Mrs. Tilghman had agreed with Elizabeth that "religion is our best hope for the reformation of the dispositions" which had pained her mother so much in Caroline's habits. She mentioned that Caroline had followed, with seeming eagerness, the common instructions of the children in spiritual reading and the catechism. If, however, Caroline should return immediately to her mother, Elizabeth hoped that Mrs. Tilghman could nevertheless find some change for the better in her daughter. That any good impressions should be lasting in a child with Caroline's turn of mind, however, seemed very uncertain to Elizabeth.

"All we can do," she wrote Mrs. Tilghman, "is to act for the best and hope in our God." After relating to Mrs. Tilghman her own harrowing experiences in becoming a Catholic, Elizabeth remarked: "Yet, the faith of the Catholic Church is the only one I can teach or advise to anyone committed to my charge."[9] In Elizabeth's experience with girls of Caroline's age (fourteen years old), the mind was sincere, unbiased and better disposed than at a later age when it so often yields to mere scepticism and indifference or to despair of anything like truth and assurance in religion.

Elizabeth was sincerely attached not only to her pupils but also to their parents and family. She wrote Mr. Matthias O'Conway:

> You know, you share with me the title of Parent, consequently the care and solicitude of that dear title must be shared and participated by a heart so fondly attached to your most dear [children] as mine is, and indeed filled with the strongest interest in your concerns.[10]

As his friend, and doubly so, Elizabeth was certain that Mr. O'Conway had no friend on earth more attached to all the family than herself. "Never till my last breath will I cease to be interested in all your concerns and every part of your ever dear family," she wrote him.[11]

Editha O'Conway was a good child possessed of simplicity and innocence. Her disposition was slow, her temper very careless, yet this was mixed with great sweetness and goodness of heart. "You must be patient as to her improvement. I am persuaded patience will remedy all," she wrote her father.[12]

Little Anna O'Conway's last letter to Elizabeth had given her hope that Mrs. O'Conway might come to Saint Joseph's for a visit and bring her daughter, Isabel. When Mrs. O'Conway and Isabel arrived excessively fatigued, Elizabeth provided comfort and quiet for them. In no time, Isabel was one of them. Elizabeth thanked Mr. O'Conway ten thousand times for sending his "better part, his most excellent and amiable Lady," and said that it was hard to express the joy and contentment the visit had given them at Saint Joseph's.

When Mr. Hughes, a mutual friend, informed Elizabeth that he had seen Mr. O'Conway pay down two hundred dollars for a picture for the chapel, the price deprived the picture of all its charms for Elizabeth. She then wrote Mr. O'Conway that if the sum he had given could be restored, then speaking as a friend to a friend, she wanted him to take it back again and wait till they both saw better financial days. Later, however, when she considered that Mr. O'Conway had given the picture to the community and not to her, she wrote: "So be it. It makes our humble chapel look really like a chapel. Our good Sisters are very proud of their present."[13] The O'Conways never had to doubt that they occupied a special place in Elizabeth's heart.

There was another family especially dear to Elizabeth Seton. For Saint Joseph's Academy was not long opened when the daughters of General and Mrs. Richard Goodloe Harper were enrolled as boarders (1811-1820) each in succession as they became of age: Diana, Mary, Elizabeth and Emily.

Diana, all affection and docility, was more than well accepted, and "as lively as the little snow birds under her feet." A French Sister, under whose care she was, made every effort to advance her in the French language. As soon as the "young lady musician" should arrive to assist them, Diana would be her first care. In the same letter, Elizabeth informed Gen. Harper that her own Anna's illness had increased to such a degree that it was no longer prudent to leave her as Diana's roommate.

Mary, the Harpers' second daughter, was cheerful and lively, but at times the unusual delicacy of her appearance and the very frequent return of a cough caused Elizabeth anxiety. On such occasions, Elizabeth notified the Harpers so that they might be acquainted with Mary's complaints and take whatever measures they thought proper. On one occasion, when Mary had a cold, she was given a "settled station" near the fire for the remainder of the winter. Also, she was provided with as much exercise as deemed necessary by Elizabeth and the Sisters.

Mary suffered, likewise, from pains in her stomach. On one occasion, Elizabeth wrote the Harpers that she had anticipated their wish that Mary take wormseed oil and the magnesia that Dr. Thomas had recommended. Twice during the winter, Mary had used the wormseed oil according to the method prescribed, and had taken her bitters made of the old wine which the Harpers had left them. For her stomach upset, Mary was given as directed a gentle dose of ipecacuanha (a plant remedy), and then the steel powders which agreed with her very well. Referring to her own children, Elizabeth wrote Mrs. Harper: "Mine have been also subject to worms at her age and older — without any consequence as they have grown up."[14]

Elizabeth seemed even more than anxious about Mary Harper's disposition than about her health. When a letter Mary had addressed to her parents was not well written, Elizabeth, not wishing to vex her, did not require her to rewrite it. Her disposition was such, however, that Elizabeth asked Mrs. Harper to write her daughter a few lines about her bad example and about the necessity of excluding her from Saint Joseph's, if she did not amend her behavior, "or anything you please provided we could obtain the end desired," she said. After receiving their letter of admonition, Mary had charmed Elizabeth so much by her improved attention to the disciplinary measures of the house that Elizabeth could not refrain from begging the Harpers to write Mary again, or to suggest to Elizabeth any means they thought proper to check "the little proud heart which becomes insupportable to her teachers."

To Gen. Harper, Elizabeth mentioned that if Mary's teachers gave her an advice gently, she would answer: "I am not speaking of that, but so or so." If they adopted a sterner stance, "she revolted openly, refused all subjection, threatened to kill herself, declared she never would behave in so vile and bad a house, though she was so good at home — and other similar extravagances which I know are nothing at her age provided we could succeed to check them," Elizabeth wrote.[15] Although every tenderness and kindness was shown Mary, Elizabeth had been sometimes obliged to confine her for some hours, and to deprive her of recreation — though always with much regret — as recreation was essential to her health which had lately improved.

The day before Mary received the second scolding letter from her father, she had been very sick. When the letter arrived, Elizabeth would not add one word to Gen. Harper's letter. "It was a moment of great tenderness on my part," she wrote him. Mary had a hard struggle reading his letter, but it soon passed. Then one day, while she was writing a letter to her father to enclose with Elizabeth's, the Sisters thought that Mary should answer his letter of admonition. "No, indeed; not one word about it," Mary replied. "And, indeed," Elizabeth remarked to Gen. Harper, "she is very silent on the subject."[16]

At times, Mary was really courageous in suppressing her temper. That, Elizabeth felt, was a great point gained. She reported to Gen Harper what his daughter had determined:

> If she were sent to Lyditz, she would stay there forever, and papa would never do anything with her by violence... and words so natural at her age — all concluding, however, with the determination to be good at Saint Joseph's the few months she is to stay.[17]

Several months later, Elizabeth again wrote the Harpers an encouraging letter. Though Mary for the moment was disappointed that her parents did not visit her, she was in perfect health, all life and spirit. She had improved considerably in every respect, except "the high haughty temper." Elizabeth was sure that for Mary's own happiness, Gen. Harper would wish the temper to be controlled. Elizabeth treated her very gently, "unless she dared them all," which sometimes happened. Then, indeed, Elizabeth could insist on her taking only bread and water for her dinner and asking pardon. That action was taken only once the long while that she was at Saint Joseph's.

Elizabeth found that Mary's emotions flashed out suddenly. But when Mary took time to reflect, which was not often, reason and good sense always predominated. For several months, now, her teachers knew that the real cause of her impatient and indocile behavior arose chiefly from an extravagant affection for the Sister who was her classroom teacher. The least attention of that Sister to any other child but Mary caused her pain.

The Harpers' third daughter, Elizabeth, was suffering from a toothache when she arrived at Saint Joseph's. Reproaching herself for not writing Gen. Harper about it earlier lest he be uneasy, Elizabeth Seton informed him that two days after he had left his daughter at Saint Joseph's, the girl's tooth still was troublesome. Dr. Moore, their dentist, had attempted to extract it, but since it was impossible to keep the girl still long enough for him to take a good hold on the tooth, he could not pull it. Elizabeth thought, however, he might have succeeded in breaking the nerve, since his daughter was quite free from pain. Elizabeth could give Gen. Harper no just reason for his daughter's pleadings, coaxing and resistance toward Dr. Moore. Perhaps the operation could be completed the next time Gen. Harper visited Saint Joseph's. "We really have not the courage to go beyond the efforts which have been made especially as the pain is past," Elizabeth wrote him.[18]

When Emily, the fourth Harper daughter, joined her sisters at Saint Joseph's several years later, Elizabeth Seton related to the General a moment of fun they had had with Emily the day before, when she was a little offended with one of her young companions and had called her a "pig." Resenting it, the girl refused to be reconciled with Emily, despite Elizabeth's entreaties. After several vain attempts of asking pardon, Emily turned away and said, "I was once [of] just such an unhappy temper myself, but my dear Papa put me in a closet and cured me, so do be patient with her."[19] Elizabeth's letters indirectly told the Harpers with what affection they were held in her heart.

A third family entered deeply into Elizabeth Seton's life through the school: Mr. and Mrs. Robert Fox of New York City. They arrived at Saint Joseph's with their three daughters: Jane, Eliza and Mary, and the "young ladies" who accompanied them. Elizabeth Seton was proud of her New Yorkers and wanted to convince Mrs. Fox that she had left her girls with friends. For their winter comfort, they would have two new stuff frocks, probably as good and as cheap in Emmitsburg as in New York.

For Elizabeth, the Fox children's mild dispositions, good behavior and family education were sufficient to recommend them. By their desire to do well, they endeared themselves more and more to all who knew them. "Never did we meet more affectionate hearts, and never among the 100's passing through our house, did we see children so generally beloved," she wrote Mr. Fox.[20]

On the day that Mr. and Mrs. Fox left them to return to New York, conquering their feelings better than Elizabeth had expected, the girls watched their parents go down the road to the last glimpse. They waited eagerly for the next week's post to know if the parents had arrived safe and well. Except for a touch of the mumps, "enough to have been confined," the girls enjoyed excellent health and spirits during their years at Saint Joseph's.

Elizabeth loved Eliza, the most affectionate of the Fox girls, next to her own daughters. On one occasion, when Eliza received letters from home, her heart showed its suffering with abundant tears. She could not look at Elizabeth without the tears starting but she would stop them quickly. Elizabeth remarked to Mrs. Fox that in her place, all she could give Eliza was a kiss.

One day, Eliza was taking a little cry at some fancy she had that all at home were not well. Jane cried because Eliza cried and Mary began to cry to keep them company, but in two minutes Elizabeth made all three laugh. She then gave them over with a little scold to her daughter, Catherine Josephine (Kitty), "who doated [sic] on them more and more." To see Jane like a mother reasoning with Eliza and to hear little Mary repeating, "Why, Eliza, they are all well," was a beautifully humorous scene for Elizabeth.[21]

When the girls were to leave Saint Joseph's at the end of the school term, Elizabeth feared that Mary, not having made her First Communion, would easily lose what she had gained at Saint Joseph's. But if she remained until the fall, she could prepare for the reception of this sacrament and later return to New York with Kitty, who, Elizabeth supposed, was going to visit her aunt, Mary Post. Elizabeth reasoned that all three of the Fox girls would then be better able to meet the challenge of this dangerous world and preserve the happy and excellent dispositions of their souls.

Knowing the Foxes' economic situation because of the extensive size of their family, Elizabeth told Mr. Fox that in Mary's case expense must not be the reason for removing her from Saint Joseph's. "We will make it [the expense] as small as you will, too happy that it should be none at all for such an object and to show our gratitude to you."[22] The Fox family had been deeply entwined with Elizabeth's heart.

Still another family entered the heart of Elizabeth: the Chatards. From the time that Elizabeth lived on Paca Street in Baltimore, Madame Marie-Françoise Chatard was one of her most intimate friends. Although they did not see each other often, Elizabeth wrote her: "I love and love you in my inmost soul."[23] Elizabeth felt, too, a special kind of gratitude toward Dr. Chatard, who attended her children and the sick Sisters in the community. In return, she loved the Chatard children, Charles and Emily, as her own, and considered them as special gifts for the future of the Church.

Away from Baltimore in Emmitsburg, Elizabeth longed to see Mrs. Chatard again and to speak her heart freely to her. "Why is the season so short in which we can hope to see you?" she wrote on one occasion. When Fr. Bruté announced from the altar that Dr. Chatard was very ill, Elizabeth wrote Mrs. Chatard that she and her community together with the children prayed continually for her husband. At Dr. Chatard's recovery, they offered their Communion in thanksgiving and joy.

Several years later, Dr. Chatard suffered a relapse. At that, Elizabeth wrote Marie-Françoise that all the community united in prayer and begged God to preserve her husband's life. Elizabeth had a feeling that Dr. Chatard might still be restored to his wife and to the thousand poor people to whom he had been a father. When she received the joyful news of his recovery, she turned her heart to God with Marie-Françoise.

Elizabeth was also fond of the Chatards' children. Quite independent of her "thousand reasons of gratitude and natural attractions" to the Chatard family, she thought that the children would eventually be very important to the Church of America. On frequent occasions, she saw Charles at Mount Saint Mary's attending the Sunday Mass and later with her own boys gathering winter nuts, the three happiest children in the world. "Your dear Charles has not yet been on the list of Infirmary Boys at the mountain," she wrote his mother.[24]

Elizabeth also related to Mrs. Chatard how one night, after Emily had fallen out of bed, Elizabeth had held her in her arms for a long time. When Emily transferred from Saint Joseph's to Madame Monroe's school in Baltimore,

Elizabeth was sure that the French system was a "thousand times better than our poor simple way" for one who was destined for society as Emily was.

But of all her Baltimore friends, Elizabeth seemed to be most at home with Mr. George Weis and his wife, Minon. Assuring Mr. Weis of her never-ending affection for him, she wrote: "You know my heart never changes to you, no, never, never."[25] She wanted him to know that if she had the power to travel, he would be the first one, after Fr. Babade, that she would ask for in Baltimore. Elizabeth never wrote George a letter that she did not include a message of love to Minon. At Mount Saint Mary's, faithful to his "master and mistress," Minon's little boy raced after every priest he saw.

In her many needs for the community, Elizabeth addressed herself most frequently to Mr. Weis. On one occasion, she begged him and Minon to receive her once more in the person of one of the Sisters for one single night. Also, if he could find an opportunity to send her the carpet she entrusted to him before they left Baltimore, it would be comfortable for Anna who was ill. On other occasions, she asked Mr. Weis for her little cabinet together with the bed to be used for Sister Rose, for a bottle of lemon juice, for some oysters for Anna and for the stove they had used in Baltimore. Then as a matter of urgency, she asked him to take a letter of special business to Gen. Harper as soon as it reached him.

These instances of Elizabeth's concern for children and parents provide a glimpse of her hopes and actions as she built her school into Christ's Kingdom on Earth. Often she accomplished this through close friendship with the parents of her students.

ABBREVIATIONS

AF to ES   - Letters from Antonio Filicchi to Elizabeth Seton.
ES to AF   - Letters from Elizabeth Seton to Antonio Filicchi.
ES to AMF   - Letters from Elizabeth Seton to Amabilia Filicchi.
ES by DeB   - *Elizabeth Seton* by Madame de Barberey.
EBS by AM   - *Elizabeth Bayley Seton* by Annabelle Melville.

LETTERS WRITTEN BY ELIZABETH SETON COMPILED IN:

LBI   - Book I
LBII   - Book II
LBIII   - Book III
LBIV   - Book IV
LBV   - Book V
LBVI   - Book VI

MEAS   - *The Life of Mrs. E.A. Seton* by Rev. Charles I. White
MLJS   - *Memoirs, Letters and Journals of Mrs. Seton*, Vol. II, by Rt. Rev. Robert Seton, D.D.
MS by GB - *Mother Seton* by Rev. Simon Gabriel Bruté.
MS to JS - *Letters of Mother Seton to Juliana Scott* by Monsignor Joseph B. Code.

END NOTES

CHAPTER 1

1. *ES* by DeB, 93; *Journal*, April 8, 1804.
2. *EBS* by AM, 137; Cheverus to Seton, March 4, 1805.
3. *MEAS* by White, C., 166 footnote.
4. *ES* by DeB, 198; Cheverus to Seton.
5. *MS to JS*, March 9, 1811, 210.
6. *LBIII*, November 10, 1812, 633; cf. Celeste, S.M., *Elizabeth Ann Seton, A Self-Portrait*, ch. 15.
7. *LBIII*, January 25, 1810, 458.
8. Carroll to Seton, March 11, 1810; Archives Saint Joseph Provincial House.
9. Scarcely two months after her conversion, Harriet, until then apparently in good health, was stricken with brain fever. On December 18, 1809, she received Holy Communion for the last time, then fell into a delirium singing hymns and calling for Fr. Babade, who had befriended her in Baltimore. She died three days before Christmas 1809. At her request, she was buried near the oak tree still standing in the Sisters' cemetery.
10. Cf., Celeste, S.M., *Elizabeth Ann Seton: A Self-Portrait*, 212-214.
11. *Ibid.*, 223-232.
12. *MS to JS*, October 25, 1818, 272.
13. *MS* by GB, 40.
14. *Ibid.*, 45.

CHAPTER 2

1. *LBI*, summer 1799, 85.
2. *ES* by DeB, June 17, 1801, 30.
3. *Diaries*, July 29, 1801, 4.
4. _____, October 2, 1800, 2.
5. _____, December 31, 1799, 1.
6. *LBV*, before August 1801, 1009.
7. *ES* by DeB, 31.
8. _____, 33.
9. *LBV*, n.d., 1060.
10. *Diaries*, January, n.d., 1803, 13.
11. *Journal*, October 28, 1803, *ESB* by DeB, 42.
12. _____, November 8, 1803, 19.
13. _____, December 4, 1803, *ES* by DeB, 62.
14. _____, December 30, 1803; _____, 74.
15. _____, May 25, 1804; _____, 97.
16. _____, December 1, 1803; _____, 60.

CHAPTER 3

1. *LBI*, February 24, 1799, 63.
2. *Ibid.*
3. *LBI*, September 10, 1799, 89.
4. ___, March 13, 1800, 111.
5. *Ibid.*, February 24, 1799, 63.
6. *LBV*, before August 17, 1801, 1021.
7. *MS to JS*, September 5, 1801, 93.
8. *Ibid.*
9. *ES* by DeB, before August 17, 1801, 36.
10. *MS to JS*, September 5, 1801, 93.
11. *LBI*, August 20, 1801, 166.
12. *MS to JS*, September 5, 1801, 93.
13. *LBI*, September, n.d., 1803, 198.

END NOTES

CHAPTER 4

1 *LBV*, before August 1801, 1009.
2 *Ibid.*, n.d., 934.
3 *ES* by DeB, August 11, 1796, 21.
4 *LBV*, n.d., 934.
5 *Ibid.*, n.d., 1055.
6 *LBI*, December 23, 1799, 97.
7 *Ibid.*
8 *LBV*, before August 1801, 1035.
9 *LBVI*, January 3, 1800, 1198.
10 *ES* by DeB, October 2, 1803, 41.
11 *Diaries*, November 19, 1803, 28.
12 *ES* by DeB, 45.
13 *Diaries*, November 20, 1803, 30.
14 *Ibid.*
15 *Ibid.*, November 21, 1803, 32.
16 *Ibid.*
17 *Ibid.*, November 24, 1803, 34.
18 ———, November 30, 1803, 39.
19 ———, November 30, 1803, 40.
20 ———, December 4, 1803, 45.
21 ———, December 12, 1803, 47.
22 ———, December 13, 1803, 49.
23 ———, December 13, 1803, 50.
24 ———, December 14, 1803, 50.
25 ———, ———, 51.
26 ———, December 20, 1803, 53.
27 ———, December 24, 1803, 54.
28 ———, December 26, 1803, 55.
29 *Ibid.*, ———.
30 *Ibid.*, ———.
31 ———, December 27, 1803, 56.
32 *Ibid.*, ———, 57.
33 *Ibid.*, ———.
34 *ES* by DeB, April 20, 1804, 95.

CHAPTER 5

1 *AF to ES*, January 9, 1804; *EBS* by AM, 114.
2 *ES to AF*, April 6, 1804; *ibid.*
3 *AF to ES, ibid.*
4 *Journal*, February 2, 1804; *ES* by DeB, 86.
5 _____, April 8, 1804; *ES* by DeB, 93.
6 _____, April 21, 1804; *ibid.*, 95.
7 *Ibid.*, _____; _____, 95-96.
8 *ES to AF*, September, n.d., 1804.
9 *Ibid.*, January 2, 1805.
10 *Ibid.*, December 13, 1804.
11 ____, August 30, 1804.
12 ____,
13 *ES to AMF*, March 25, 1805; *ES* by DeB, 142.
14 *ES to AF*, April 18, 1820.

CHAPTER 6

1 *MS to JS*, November 25, 1798, 43.
2 *Ibid.*
3 *LBV*, n.d., 1017.
4 *LBI*, March 11, 1801, 147.
5 *ES* by DeB, 64; *Journal*, December 1803.
6 *ES* by DeB, 60; *Journal*, December 1, 1803.
7 *Ibid.*, 91; _____, April 5, 1804.
8 *Ibid.*, 101; _____, July 8, 1804.

CHAPTER 7

1 *MS to JS*, April 16, 1798, 15.
2 *Ibid.*, November 19, 1800, 79.
3 ____, January 3, 1799, 46.
4 ____, October 28, 1798, 39.
5 ____, June 1801, 90.

6 ———, August 19, 1802, 101.
7 ———, June 1801, 90.
8 ———, January 7, 1802, 97.
9 ———, Sunday, p.m., n.d., 1803, 107.
10 ———, May 9, 1798, 20.
11 ———, June 1801, 90.
12 ———, January 7, 1802, 98.
13 ———, November 25, 1798, 43.
14 ———, March 18, 1800, 72.
15 *LBI*, August 11, 1796, 11.
16 *MS to JS*, May 14, 1799, 58.
17 ————, October 6, 1798, 26.
18 ————, December 7, 1800, 80.
19 ————, June 3, 1798, 25.
20 ————, November 16, 1802, 104.
21 ————, January 20, 1799, 50.
22 ————, March 8, 1808, 160.

CHAPTER 8

1 *LBI*, April 8, 1803, 193.
2 *Ibid.*, October 1, 1803, 201.
3 *LBV*, n.d., 959.
4 *ES to AF*, August 10, 1806.
5 *LBV*, n.d., 978.
6 *MS to JS*, July 20, 1807, 150.
7 *LBII*, August 14, 1807, 310.
8 *Diaries*, September 18, 1807, 102.
9 *Ibid.*, October 16, 1807, 106.
10 *LBV*, n.d., 958.
11 *Ibid.*, n.d., 997.
12 *LBII*, August 15, 1807, 310.
13 Luke 18:1.
14 *LBV*, n.d., 967.
15 *Ibid.*, n.d., 958.
16 ———, n.d., 968.

17 *MLJS*, Vol. II, June 28, 1808, 23.
18 A benevolent convert, the Rev. Mr. Sutherland Cooper, studying for the priesthood wished to further Elizabeth's plans for building a school and founding a sisterhood. For this purpose, he purchased the Fleming Farm in Emmitsburg, Maryland, in trust to Elizabeth Seton. Cf. Sister Marie Celeste, *Elizabeth Ann Seton: A Self-Portrait*, Ch. 11, 3, 279.
19 *MLJS*, March 26, 1809, 49.
20 *LBIII*, June 23, 1809, 425.
21 *MEAS*, White, C., 277.
22 During their sojourn at Mount Saint Mary's, Elizabeth's sister-in-law, Harriet, made her decision to become a Catholic on the feast of Saint Mary Magdalene, July 22, 1809, a decision she hesitated to make while with her Protestant relatives. Two months later on September 24, she made her First Communion at the hands of Fr. Pierre Babade who was dearly loved by Elizabeth and her household. In the last week of November, Harriet was stricken with brain fever. She received Communion for the last time on December 18. In her delirium the next four days, she sang hymns and called for Fr. Babade. She died on December 22, 1809, and was buried near the oak tree which still stands in the Sisters' cemetery in Saint Joseph's Valley.
23 *MEAS*, White, C., 279.

CHAPTER 9

1 *LBIV*, August 21, 1818, 874.
2 *Ibid.*
3 *LBII*, June 20, 1808, 371.
4 *Ibid.*, 370.
5 _____, 371.
6 *LBIII*, September 14, 1812, 618.
7 *Ibid.*, n.d., 542.
8 *LBIII*, March, n.d., 1814, 673.
9 *Ibid.*, March 8, 1810, 465.

END NOTES

10 ____, ____.
11 ____, May 6, 1810, 478.
12 ____, November 21, 1810, 525.
13 ____, May 12, 1811, 553.
14 ____, August 2, 1812, 613.
15 ____, ____.
16 ____, September 14, 1812, 617.
17 ____, September 17, 1813, 657.
18 ____, November 10, 1812, 634.
19 *LBV*, n.d., 1077.
20 *ES to AF*, July 1, 1814.
21 *LBIII*, November 21, 1810, 525.
22 *LBV*, n.d., 1081.
23 ____, n.d., 1083.
24 ____, n.d., 1086.
25 ____, March 1814, 673.
26 ____, n.d., 1083.
27 ____, n.d., 1082.
28 ____, n.d., 1080.

CHAPTER 10

1 Simon William Gabriel Bruté de Remur was born of a noble family at Rennes in the province of Normandy, France on March 20, 1779. He was graduated with highest honor from the University of Paris, School of Medicine where he defended his dissertation. When he felt God was calling him to a priestly vocation, he began the study of theology at the Seminary of Saint Sulpitius in Paris. After his ordination, he joined the Society of Saint Sulpitius to become a missionary. In 1810, he accompanied the Right Reverend Benedict Flaget who had been appointed Bishop of Bardstown, Kentucky, and who was returning to Baltimore, Maryland, with the rules of the Daughters of Charity of Saint Vincent de Paul. Cf. White, Charles, *MEAS*, 334.

2 *LBIII*, August 9, 1811, 505.

3 *Ibid.*, Christmas 1811, 588.
4 *EBS* by AM, 297; 454, note 17.
5 *MS* by GB, n.d., 46.
6 *Ibid.*, 136-137.
7 *EBS* by AM, 295; 453, note 7.
8 *Ibid.*, 298; 454, note 24.
9 *MS* by GB, n.d., 45.
10 *Ibid.*, n.d., 41.
11 *MS* by GB, n.d., 48.
12 *MEAS* by White, C., 434.
13 *EBS* by AM, 319; 459, note 123.
14 *MS* by GB, n.d., 21.
15 *LBIV*, n.d., 1815, 708.
16 *MLJS*, 188.
17 *Ibid.*, 195-196.
18 *LBIV*, fall 1815, 739.
19 *EBS* by AM, 307.
20 *Ibid.*, 306; 455, note 53.
21 *Diaries*, 132.
22 *Ibid.*, 144.
23 ____, 145.
24 *LBIV*, fall 1815, 739.
25 ____, September 2, 1816, 787.
26 ____, August 1, 1817.
27 *LBV*, Transfiguration, n.d., 1104.
28 *LBIV*, n.d., 841.
29 *Ibid.*, fall 1815, 709.
30 *MLJS*, n.d., 1816, 216.
31 *Ibid.*, 218-219.
32 *Ibid.*, summer 1816, 232.
33 *LBV*. Seton to Bruté, n.d., 1094.
34 *LBIV*, September 2, 1816, 788.
35 *Ibid.*, June 4, 1817, Trinity Sunday, 821.
36 *EBS* by AM, 322.
37 *LBIV*, September, 1818-1819, 876.
38 *LBV*, n.d., 1095.

39 "The Sisters of Charity in this country . . . owe a debt of gratitude to [Bruté]. Mother Seton found in him an enlightened director and friend, and his advice and influence was most beneficial to her young community at Saint Joseph's." Cf. *MLJS*, Vol. II, 136; cf. footnote: Memoirs of Simon G. Bruté.

40 *MEAS*, White, C., 442.

The following notice was found among Bruté's papers on Mother Seton: "In the first place, I will say as the result of my long and intimate acquaintances with her, that I believe her to have been one of those truly chosen souls (*âmes d'élite*), who, if placed in circumstances similar to those of St. Theresa or St. Frances de Chantal, would be equally remarkable in the scale of sanctity. For it seems to me impossible that there could be a greater elevation, purity, and love for God, for heaven and for supernatural and eternal things than were to be found in her." Cf. *MEAS*, White, C., 512.

APPENDIX

1 *LBIV*, fall 1815, 739.
2 *Ibid*.
3 *LBIII*, n.d., 577.
4 *MS to JS*, May 30, 1810, 200.
5 *Ibid*., March 9, 1811, 211.
6 *LBIII*, November 6, 1811, 579.
7 *LBV*, n.d., 1171.
8 *Ibid*.
9 *LBIV*, January 1820, 912.
10 *LBIII*, February 20, 1810, 460.
11 *LBV*, n.d., 434.
12 *LBIII*, February 20, 1810, 461.
13 *Ibid*., June 5, 1810, 495.
14 ____, March (before 6th) 1814, 667.
15 ____, October 15, 1814, 680.

16 ____, December 6, 1814, 685.
17 ____, _____.
18 *LBIV*, January 26, 1817, 810.
19 *LBVI*, January 1, 1820, 1313.
20 *LBIV*, October 10, 1817, 838.
21 *LBVI*, September 8, 1816, 1258.
22 ____, May 9, 1818, 1289.
23 *LBIII*, November 6, 1811, 579.
24 *Ibid.*, _____.
25 ____, December 6, 1812, 635.
26 *LBVI*, January 24, 1810, 1125.
27 *LBV*, n.d., 1817 [?], 1138-39.

A SELECTED BIBLIOGRAPHY

Primary Sources:

1. *Manuscripts*

The Book of Diaries

Books of Letters
    Books I-VI (chronological order)

The First Book of Instructions

The Second Book of Instructions

Books of Translations:
    Book   I The Life of Mr. Vincent
    Book II The Life of Madame Le Gras
                Excerpts from the Life Of Ignatius of Loyola
    Book III Interior Peace by Ambroise de Lombez

Typescript copies of Elizabeth Ann Seton's manuscripts obtained from the Sacred Congregation for the Causes of the Saints in Rome were authorized by the late Reverend Charles-Léon Souvay, C.M. These are now preserved in the Archives of the Sisters of Charity at Seton Hill, Greensburg, Pennsylvania.

2. Annotated Personal Books

The Holy Bible. First American Edition. Philadelphia: Mathew Carey, 1805. Gift of Antonio Filicchi. Rare Books Collection at Notre Dame University, Indiana.

Commentary on the Book of Psalms by George, Lord Bishop of Norwich, Oxford, printed by William Young, Philadelphia, 1792. Gift of the Reverend John Hobart, June 17, 1802. Bruté Memorial Library, Vincennes, Indiana.

The Following of Christ by Thomas á Kempis. Translated into English by the Rt. Rev. Richard Challoner, D.D. Philadelphia: Mathew Carey, 1800. Archives of the Sisters of Charity, Seton Hill, Greensburg, Pennsylvania.

Prayer Book. No title or author: published before 1816. Robert Seton collection, Archives of Notre Dame University, Indiana. Gift of Bishop Cheverus of Boston.

3. *French books in Elizabeth Seton's possession at her death borrowed from the library of the Reverend Simon G. Bruté now preserved in the Bruté Memorial Library in Vincennes, Indiana.*

(Asterisks indicate the books, portions of which Elizabeth Seton translated into English.)

Author not given. *Relation abrégée de la vie de Madame de Combé.* Institutrice de la Maison du Bon Pasteur. Paris: Florentin et Pierre Delaune, 1700.

* Abelly, Louis (Evêque de Rodez). *La vie du vénérable serviteur de dieu, Vincent de Paul.* Paris: Florentin Lambert, 1664.

_____. *La conduite de l'Eglise Catholique touchant le culte du très saint sacrement de l'Eucharistie.* Paris: Veuve Georges Jossé, 1678.
* Andilly, Arnauld d'. *Oeuvres de Sainte-Thérèsa.* Traduites en français pas A. d'Andilly. Paris: Denys Thierry, 1687.
* Avrillon, Jean-Baptiste (Rev.). *Conduite pour passer saintemente le temps de l'avent.* Marseille: Jean Mossy, 1811.
* Berthier, Guillaume-François (S.J.) *Les psaumes traduits en franqis avec des notes et des réflexions.* Paris: Adrien Le Clère, 1807.

_____. *Réflexions spirituelles*, Tomes I-V. Paris: Mérigot le Jeune, 1790. Nouvelle éd. Toulouse: Simon Sacarau, 1811.

_____. *Oeuvres spirituelles.* Nouvelle éd. Paris: Adrien Le Clère, 1811.

Boudon, Henry-Marie (Rev.) *La vie cachée avec Jésu en Dieu.* Paris: Estienne Michallet, 1691.

_____. *La conduite de la divine providence et l'adoration perpetuelle.* Paris: Estienne Michallet, 1678.

* Bouhours, Dominique (S.J.) *La vie de Saint Ignace, fondateur de la compagnie de Jésus.* Paris: Mabre-Cramoisy, 1679.

Collet, Pierre (C.M.). *La vie de Saint Vincent de Paul.* Nouvelle éd. Lyon: Rusand, 1811.

Crasset, Jean (S.J.) *La douce et sainte mort.* Paris: Estienne Michallet, 1681.

* de Bonrecueil, Joseph Duranti (Rev.) *Les oeuvres de Saint Ambroise sur la virginité.* Paris: Barthelemy Alix, 1729.
* de Lombez, Ambroise (O.F.M. Cap.). *Traité de la paix intérieure.* Paris: Guillot, 1766.

_____. *Lettres spirituelles sur la paix intérieure et autres sujets de piété.* Paris: Guillot, 1776.

* du Point, Louis (S.J.) *Méditations sur les mystères de la foy*. Traduites de l'espagnol par Jean Brignon, S.J. Tomes I, III, IV. Paris: François Muguet, 1683, 1684, 1689; Tomes I et VI, Paris: Jean de Nully, 1708.
* François de Sales, Saint. *Epîtres spiritueles*, recueillies par M. Louys de Sales (neveu). Lyon: Vincent de Coeursilly, Paris: Sebastien Hure, 1625.
———. *Sermons*, recueillis par les religieuses de la Visitation Saints Marie d'Annecy. Second éd. Paris: 1643.
———. *Lettres circulaires aux communautés des religieuses de la Visitation Sainte-Marie*. Paris: 1655.
———. *Introduction á la vie dévote de Saint François de Sales*. Nouvelle éd. par Jean Brignon, S.J. Lyon: Le Frères Bruyset, 1746.
* Gobillon, Nicolas. *La vie de Mademoiselle Le Gras, fondatrice et première superiéure de la Compagnie des Filles de la Charité*. Paris: Pralard, 1676.

Huby, Vincent (S.J.). *Oeuvres spirituelles*. Paris: Gabrielle-Charles Berton, 1758.

Jegou, Jean (S.J.) *La préparation à la mort*. Rennes: François Vatar, 1688; Nicolas Devaux, 1733.

* Judde, Claude (S.J.) *Retraite spirituelle pour les personnes religieuses*. Paris: Gissey et Bordelet, 1746.

Lallemant, Louis (S.J.) *La doctrine spirituelle du Père Louis Lallemant* . . . précédée de sa vie par Pierre Champion, S.J. Paris: Estienne Michallet, 1694.

La Vallière, Louise Françoise (Madame la duchesse de). *Réflexions sur la miséricorde de Dieu*. Paris: Etienne-François Savoye, 1744.

Nicole, Pierre. *Essais de morale* . . . contenant des réflexions morales sur les Epîtres et Evangiles. Paris: Guillaume Desprez et Jean Dessartz, 1713.

Saint-Jure, Jean Baptiste (S.J.). *Méditations . . . de la foy*. Paris: Pierre le Petit, 1654.

_____. *Le Maistre Jésus Christ.* Paris: La Veuve Jean Camusat et Pierre le Petit, 1649.

_____. *Le livre des élus.* Paris: La Veuve Jean Camusat. 1643.

Surin, Jean-Joseph (S.J.). *Les fondements de la vie spirituelle tirés du livre de l'Imitation de Jésus-Christ.* Paris: Cramoisy, 1667, Nouvelle éd. revue et corrigée par Jean Brignon, S.J., 1703.

_____. *Dialogues spirituels choisis où la perfection chrétienne est expliquée pour toutes les personnes.* Tome II. Troisiéme éd. Paris: Edmé Couterot, 1719.

* Vincent de Paul, Saint. *Conférences spirituelles pour l'explication des règles des Soeur de Charité.* Paris: Demonville, 1803.

References:

1. Books

Angeli, Roberto. *Elisabetta Anna Seton, la donna della speranza.* A cura della Postulazione Generale, C.M., Roma, 1975.

Bruté, Rev. Simon G. *Mother Seton,* notes from the original papers in the possession of the Daughters of Charity Motherhouse, Emmitsburg, Maryland, 1884.

Celeste, Sister Marie, S.C. *Elizabeth Ann Seton: A Self-Portrait; A Study of Her Spirituality in Her Own Words.* Foreword by Bernard Basset, S.J. Libertyville, IL: Franciscan Marytown Press, 1986.

Code, Joseph B. *Letters of Mother Seton to Mrs. Juliana Scott.* New York: Burgio Memorial Foundation, 1960.

Cushing, Richard Cardinal. *Blessed Mother Seton.* Pictorial biography. Boston: Saint Paul Editions, 1963.

Danemarie, Jeanne. *Une fille américaine de Monsieur Vincent.* Paris: Editions Spes, 1950.

De Barberey, Mme. Hélène. *Elizabeth Seton.* Translated from the sixth French edition by the Rt. Rev. Msgr. Joseph B. Code. Emmitsburg, Maryland: Mother Seton Guild Press, 1957.

Dirvin, Joseph I. (C.M.) *Mrs. Seton: Foundress of the American Sisters of Charity.* New York: Farrar, Straus and Giroux, 1962; rev. ed., 1975.

Melville, Annabelle. *Elizabeth Bayley Seton.* New York: Charles Scribner's Sons, 1951; rev. ed. St. Paul, Minn.: Carillon Books, 1976.

Poisenet, Marie-Dominique. *Elizabeth Seton. Je ne cherche que Dieu et son église.* Paris: Editions Saint Paul, 1967.

Power-Waters, Alma. *Mother Seton and the Sisters of Charity,* New York: Vision Books, a division of Farrar, Straus, Inc. Published simultaneously in Toronto, Canada. Ambassador Books, Ltd., 1957.

Reville, John E. (S.J.) *Mother Seton.* Second ed. New York: The American Press, 1921.

Seton, Rt. Rev. Robert. *Memoir, Letters and Journal of Elizabeth Seton.* New York: P. O'Shea, 1869.

White, Charles I. (Rev.) *Life of Mrs. Eliza A. Seton.* New York: Edward Dunigan and Brother, 1853.

2. *General Works*

Bruté de Rémur, Simon Guillaume Gabriel. *Selected Writings of Simon G. Bruté.* Edited by the Reverend Thomas G. Smith, S.T.D. Emmitsburg, Maryland: Mount Saint Mary's Seminary, 1977.

De Andrada, F. Thomas of Jesus. *The Sufferings of Our Lord Jesus Christ.* Translated from Portuguese. Dublin: P. Wogan, 1794; Westminster, MD, Newman Press, [1960].

Derrick, Christopher. *The Delicate Creation; Towards a Theology of the Environment.* Foreword by René Dubos. Intro. by John Cardinal Wright. Old Greenwich, Conn.: Devin-Adair Co., 1972.

Faricy, Robert L. *Seeking Jesus in Contemplation and Discernment.* Wilmington: Michael Glazier, 1983.

Hassel, David J., S.J. *Dark Intimacy. Hope For Those in Difficult Prayer-Experiences.* New York/Mahwah: Paulist Press, 1986.

Hinnebush, Paul. *Friendship in the Lord.* Notre Dame, Indiana: Ave Maria Press, 1974.

Kiesling, Christopher. *Celibacy, Prayer and Friendship: A Making-Sense-Out-Of-Life Approach.* New York: Alba House, 1978.

Maloney, George A. *Journey into Contemplation.* Locust Valley, N.Y.: Living Flame Press, 1983.

Scupoli, Lorenzo. *The Spiritual Combat and A Treatise on Peace of Soul.* A translation. Revised by William Lester and Robert Mohan. New York: Paulist Press, 1978.

Van Kaam, Adrian L. and Muto, Susan A. *Practicing the Prayer of Presence.* First English edition. Denville, N.J.: Dimension Books, 1980.

---

* For additional bibliographic entries cf: *Elizabeth Ann Seton: A Self-Portrait; A Study of Her Spirituality in Her Own Words*, by Sister Marie Celeste, S.C. Libertyville, IL 60048: Franciscan Marytown Press, 1986.

INDEX

Academy of Sculpture, Florence, 72.
Annunziata, Church of the, Florence, 72.
Babade, Rev. Pierre, S.S., in Baltimore, MD, 12; favorite spiritual director, 17; interested in Elizabeth Seton's community, 142; befriends Elizabeth, 165; influences Elizabeth Seton's educational enterprise, 166; close friendship with Elizabeth Seton, 167.
Baltimore, Maryland, Seton School, 12; Saint Mary's College, 10; Saint Mary's Chapel, 12; Cecilia Seton's death in, 127.
Barclay, Charlotte Amelia, second wife of widowed Doctor Richard Bayley, 3; step-mother of Elizabeth Bayley Seton, 3; taught Elizabeth Bayley twenty-second Psalm, 22; attended at death bed by Elizabeth Bayley Seton, 16.
Bayley, Emma Craig, half-sister of Elizabeth Seton, 15; taught prayers by Elizabeth Seton, 22; Elizabeth Seton at death bed of, 16.
Bayley, Guy Carleton, half-brother of Elizabeth Seton, 8, 60; at wharf in Leghorn, 52; in Pisa with Setons, 65; kept watch at William Seton's death in Pisa, 65.
Bayley, Dr. Joseph, associate of Dr. Richard Bayley, 42; assists at burial of Dr. Richard Bayley, 42; at Staten Island quarantine, 44.
Bayley, Dr. Richard LeConte, father of Elizabeth Bayley Seton and first friend, 3, 33; studies in London, 4, 22, 33; opens Staten Island Health Establishment, 4, 34; achieves fame, 4, 37; cares for yellow fever victims, 5, 38, 39; deeply loves Elizabeth Seton and her children, 34, 35; authors article in *Monitor* on yellow fever, 36, 37; untiring service at quarantine, 38; loves music, 37, 38; falls victim to yellow fever, 40; Elizabeth Seton's care of, 38, 39, 41; illness and death of, 41, 42; burial in Saint Andrew's Churchyard, 42; Elizabeth Seton's gratitude to Dr. Moore, 42; inscription on tombstone, 43.
Bayley, William LeConte, brother of Dr. Richard Bayley, 3; owns farm in New Rochelle, 22; Elizabeth Bayley meets cousins and French relatives at her uncle's farm, 3; learns to love nature, 23, 33.
Besley, Madame Olivier, Elizabeth Bayley's French relative, 3; confides her eldest son to Elizabeth Seton, 35; interest in Dr. Bayley's pursuits, 37, 38.

Blooming Rose, ship boarded by Fr. Bruté returning to Baltimore from Bordeaux, France, 149.
Bourdaloue, Rev. Louis, S.J., French Jesuit priest and a favorite author of Elizabeth Seton, 85; religious influence on Elizabeth Seton, 85, 86.
Boyle, Betsey, Sister of Charity, 18, 156.
Bruté, Rev. Simon Gabriel, S.S., early years in France, 189; French missionary, 141; Elizabeth Seton's priest friend, 15, 142; "Angel of the Mountain," 15; first meeting with Elizabeth Seton, 141; director of Saint Mary's Seminary, 141; engaged in adapting French rules, 141; forms lasting friendship with Elizabeth Seton, 141; interest in Elizabeth Seton's community, 142; interest in Seton's children, 142, 152; learns of Annina's consecration to God, 142; at Annina's death bed, 142; comforts Elizabeth Seton, 143; nick-named "Seraphim," 143; librarian at Mount St. Mary's College, 145; appointed president of St. Mary's College, 147; prepares for a voyage to France, 147; accompanies William Seton to Europe, 147; tries to fulfill his trust to Elizabeth, 148; writes to Mr. Preudhomme de Borre in behalf of William Seton, 148; returns to Baltimore, 149; assumes presidency at St. Mary's, 150; missed in Emmitsburg, 150, 151; encouraged by Elizabeth, 151; visited by French missionaries, 152; particular interest in Rebecca Seton, 153, 154; Rebecca's love for, 154; at Rebecca's death bed, 154; brought Holy *Viaticum* to Rebecca, 154; Elizabeth's advice on how to treat parents, 165, 166; desires to return to Emmitsburg mountains, 155; reappointed assistant to Father DuBois, 155; letter to Elizabeth Seton, 156; called to Elizabeth Seton's sick bed, 157; administers Sacrament of Healing, 157; visits Elizabeth Seton frequently during her illness, 157; prays with Sisters, 157; celebrates Eucharistic liturgy at Elizabeth's funeral, 158; poetic lines in memory of Elizabeth Seton, 158; note on Mother Seton's life, 191; created Bishop of Vincennes, Indiana, 158; death of, 158.
Butler, Alban, *Lives of the Saints*, 77.
Butler, Mary Ann, Sister of Charity, 12.
Carroll, Archbishop John, Bishop of Baltimore, learns about Elizabeth Seton, 9; confirms Elizabeth Seton, 9; approves DuBourg's plan for Elizabeth Seton, 10; upholds Elizabeth Seton as superior of sisters, 15.
Cartelach, Doctor, William Magee Seton's physician in Pisa, 65.
Charlton, Catherine Bayeux, mother of Elizabeth Ann Bayley, wife of Dr. Richard Bayley, 3.
Chatard, Madame Marie Françoise, wife of Dr. Pierre Chatard, Baltimore friend of Elizabeth Seton, 17, 165, 167; Elizabeth's fondness for children of, 177, 178.
Chatard, Dr. Pierre, famed French physician, 16; attends Cecilia Seton in Baltimore, 127; attends Rebecca Seton, 16; attending physician at St. Joseph's, 177; illness of, 178; prayers for recovery of, 178.

INDEX

Cheverus, Rev. John, first Bishop of Boston, friend of Antonio Filicchi, 9; receives letter from Elizabeth Seton, 9; advice to Elizabeth Seton, 9; approves DuBourg's plan for Elizabeth Seton, 11; esteemed by Elizabeth Seton, 137.

Clossy, Susan, Sister of Charity, 12.

Cooper, Samuel Sutherland, seminarian convert, befriends Elizabeth Seton, 15; purchased Fleming Farm as gift to Elizabeth Seton, 12; fosters plans for Elizabeth's pursuits, 166, 188.

David, Rev. John, S.S., Sulpician friend of Fr. Bruté, 143.

de Andreis, Rev. Felix, C.M., friend of Fr. Bruté, led a group of missionaries to Emmitsburg, 152.

DeLanceys, wealthy New York friends of Dr. Bayley and Setons, 4; first meeting of Elizabeth Bayley and William Magee Seton at home of, 45.

DuBois, Rev. John, S.S., founder of Mount Saint Mary's College, 13, 127; greets Elizabeth and group, 13; last named superior of infant community, 15; director of Elizabeth Seton's sisterhood, 144; helps set tone for Elizabeth's school, 167, 168; administers Sacrament of Healing to Elizabeth Seton, 18.

DuBourg, Rev. William Valentine, S.S., president of Saint Mary's College, 10, 125; meets Elizabeth Seton in New York, 10; invites Elizabeth to Baltimore, 10; receives letter from Elizabeth en route to Emmitsburg, 127; Sulpician friend of Fr. Bruté, 143; Fr. Cheverus approves plans for Elizabeth Seton, 11.

Duhamel, Rev. Charles, S.S., pastor at Saint Joseph's Church, 150; letter to Elizabeth Seton about Father Bruté, 150.

DuPavillon, Charles, student at St. Mary's College, Baltimore, romance with Anna Maria Seton, 133.

Dupleix, Catherine (Dué), New York friend of Elizabeth Seton, 11; loves Elizabeth Seton's children, 132; defends Elizabeth Seton to Protestant friends, 87, 130; member of Widow's Society, 129; invited to Emmitsburg, 130, 134; dislikes letter writing, 131; enjoys hearing about Seton children, 131, 132; sufferings change to joy, 132; Dué's conversion, 125, 136; welcomed to Saint Joseph, 135; at Mrs. Chatard's, 136; enjoys peace and love, 136.

Farquhar, Eliza Curson, William Magee Seton's aunt and early friend of Elizabeth Seton; Seton's breakfast at home of, 93.

Filicchi, Amabilia, wife of Antonio Filicchi; befriends Elizabeth Seton, 7, 71; Mass at Santa Catarina, 8, 76; kindness of, 75; at William Magee Seton's death, 69; accompanies Elizabeth to Florence, 71, 74; practices Catholic faith and beliefs, 7, 75; suggests that Antonio accompany Elizabeth Seton to New York, 76; bids farewell to Setons, 8, 77; plans Elizabeth's and Annina's tour of Florence, 7, 71.

Filicchi, Antonio, friend of William Magee Seton, 5; awaits arrival of Setons in Leghorn, 6, 52; disappointed at detention in Lazaretto, 6, 52; befriends Elizabeth, 6, 73; teaches Elizabeth how to make the sign of the cross, 6, 76;

welcomes Setons to his home, 7, 69; delay deemed providential, 7; accompanies Setons to New York, 8, 76; comforts Willian Seton in Lazaretto, 53, 56; visits William with Doctor Tutilli, 56; accompanies Rev. Mr. Hall to Lazaretto, 61; visits William Seton with Captain O'Brien, 66; instructs Elizabeth on faith, 76, 77; friendship with Elizabeth deepens, 77; leaves for Boston, 79; gives Elizabeth book *Jesus Psalter*, 84; sponsors Elizabeth in the Catholic Church, 86; promises to call for Elizabeth in Garden of Paradise, 86; returns to Leghorn, 88; introduces Elizabeth Seton to Father Cheverus, 85.

Filicchi Family, Elizabeth Seton's first Catholic friends, 5; provide comfort for Setons in Lazaretto, 53, 55, 56; escort Setons to Pisa, 6, 64; take Elizabeth to the Shrine of *La Madonna delle Grazie* in Montenero, 75; welcome Setons again in their home, 75.

Filicchi, Filippo, business friend of William Magee Seton, 5; at Leghorn Habor, 6; challenges Elizabeth to pray and inquire into the Catholic faith, 7; throws out last challenge to Elizabeth, 77; bids Elizabeth farewell on her return to America, 77; interested in converting Elizabeth to Catholicism, 71; gave Elizabeth a copy of *Introduction to the Devout Life*, 84; approves plan that Antonio escort Elizabeth to America, 76; Elizabeth's esteem for, 77; last blessing to Elizabeth at Leghorn Harbor, 77.

Filicchi, Mary Cowper, wife of Filippo Filicchi; escorts the Setons to Pisa, 6, 64; plans Elizabeth's tour of Florence, 7, 71; greets Setons at Lazaretto, 53; at William Seton's death, 69.

Flaget, Rev. Benedict, Bishop of Bardstown, Kentucky; friend of Fr. Bruté, 143.

Florence, tour of, 71, 72.

Following of Christ by Thomas à Kempis, translated from Latin, *Imitatio Christi*, 9, 60, 84.

Fox, Mr. Robert, New York friend of Elizabeth Seton; enrolls daughters at St. Joseph's Academy, 176; Elizabeth's special interest in children of, 177.

George, Margaret, Sister of Charity, superior at New York, 131, 156.

Georgetown College, Maryland, 10.

Grand Sachem, a packet, Elizabeth Seton and daughters board, 125; leaves New York Harbor, 125; arrives in Baltimore, 125.

Hall, Rev. Mr. Thomas, Protestant minister in Leghorn, visits William Magee Seton in Lazaretto, 61; presides at funeral services of William M. Seton, 69.

Harper, Robert Goodloe, Major General United States Army, enrolled daughters at St. Joseph's Academy, 172; receives reports from Elizabeth Seton, 173, 175; wrote scolding letters to daughter Mary, 174.

Harris, William, Episcopalian clergyman, headmaster of school in New York, 10.

Hobart, Rev. John Henry, Episcopalian minister at Trinity Church, New York, friend of William and Elizabeth Seton, 8, 11, 62, 94; sends affectionate note to Elizabeth, 81; recommends Newton's *Prophecies*, 82; opposes Elizabeth's conversion, 82.

INDEX

Huler, Mammy, assists Elizabeth with household chores, 107; illness of, 95; death of, 114.
Hurley, Rev. Michael, O.S.A., friend of Elizabeth Seton, assistant at St. Peter's Church, New York City, 11; at Saint Mary's Chapel, Baltimore, 12; receives Cecilia Seton into the Church at St. Peter's, 119; offers Mass, 123.
Kohlman, Rev. Anthony, S.J., spiritual director of Cecilia Seton, 125.
La Madonna delle Grazie, shrine of Our Lady in Montenero, Italy, visited by Elizabeth Seton and Filicchis, 75; Elizabeth's belief in the Eucharist, 75.
Lazaretto, at Staten Island, 34; at Leghorn, 6, 52, 54, 56, 62-64, 68.
Leghorn, Italy, Setons journey to, 5, 50.
Liberties, Seton ship docked in New York Harbor, 98; victory party, 98.
Louis, Lazaretto man-servant provided by the Filicchis, 55; kept watch at William's death, 68.
Maitland, Eliza Seton, half-sister of William Magee Seton, illness of, 97; infant of, 108; Elizabeth Seton at death bed of, 16.
Maitland, James, partner of Seton-Maitland firm, 5; suspends operations in London and Hamburg, 49; bankruptcy, 49.
Matignon, Rev. Francis A., friend of Fr. Cheverus of Boston, 9; approves DuBourg's plan for Elizabeth Seton, 11, 85.
Medici Palace, Florence, Italy, 71.
Memorare, Saint Bernard's prayer to Our Lady, 83.
Montenero, site of shrine visited by Elizabeth, 7; in shrine chapel at Mass, Elizabeth receives the gift of faith in real presence of Jesus, 7, 76.
Monti Morelli, mountains viewed from the Medici Palace, Florence, 71.
Montreal, Canada, Elizabeth plans family move to, 10; schooling for her sons, 10.
Moore, Dr. Richard Channing, pastor at Richmond, Staten Island, 42; burial services for Dr. Richard Bayley, 42; Elizabeth's letter to, 42.
Mount St. Mary's, Emmitsburg, Elizabeth Seton and community, greeted by Rev. John DuBois, 13, 14, 141; William and Richard transferred to college, 14; Harriet Seton converted at, 188:22; Bruté returns to, 156.
Murphy, Maria, joins Elizabeth Seton's Community in Baltimore, 12; sets out for Emmitsburg, 126; funeral of, 144.
Murray, Messrs. John and Sons, creditors of Antonio Filicchi, 10; Antonio Filicchi authorizes funds to meet Elizabeth Seton's needs, 10.
New Rochelle, French Huguenot settlement, 3; Dr. Bayley sends Elizabeth to, 33; forms close friendships with cousins and relatives in, 3, 33; in Leghorn Lazaretto, Elizabeth reminisces her experiences with Cousin Joe of, 57.
New York City, Elizabeth Seton's birthplace, 3; Setons sail from, 5, 51; yellow fever epidemic in, 38, 39, 97; Elizabeth returns to, 8; embraces Catholicism in, 9, 86; Elizabeth meets Rev. DuBourg in, 10; Setons leave relatives and friends in, 11.
O'Brien, Captain of the *Shepherdess*, 52; visits William M. Seton, 59-60, 66; refuses Setons return passage to New York, 75.

O'Brien, Rev. Matthew in New York, pastor of Saint Peter's Church, 9, 95; delighted Elizabeth Seton, 85; receives Elizabeth Seton into Church, 86.

O'Conway, Cecilia, friend of Father Babade, joins Elizabeth's community in Baltimore, 12; at Elizabeth Seton's deathbed, 18.

O'Conway, Matthias, father of Cecilia O'Conway, friend of Elizabeth Seton, 17, 169; receives letter from Elizabeth Seton, 170; donated picture for chapel, 171; Elizabeth's attachment to family of, 171.

Paca Street, Baltimore, site of Elizabeth Seton's new home and first school, 12; Elizabeth begins religious community on, 12; Harriet and Cecilia's arrival at, 12, 126; Elizabeth leaves Paca Street for Emmitsburg, 13, 127.

Philadelphia, Babade recuits candidates for Elizabeth Seton's community in, 12; Rebecca Seton goes to, 16, 153; Julia Scott invited Elizabeth to visit her in, 16.

Physick, Doctor, Philadelphia specialist, attends Rebecca Seton, 116.

Pitti Palace, Florence, visited by Elizabeth and Annina Seton, 71.

Plunkett, Abbé Peter, Irish priest in Leghorn, introduced to Elizabeth Ann Seton, 71.

Pope Paul VI, canonized Elizabeth Ann Seton, 19.

Post, Mary Magdalen Bayley, sister of Elizabeth Bayley Seton and wife of Dr. Wright Post, 4; Elizabeth and William M. Seton married in home of, 4, 46; cared for infant Rebecca Seton, during Elizabeth Seton's sojourn in Leghorn, 5; cared for Anna Maria and William Seton during Doctor Bayley's illness, 41; at Dr. Bayley's death bed, 49.

Post, Dr. Wright, husband of Mary Magdalen Bayley, 46, 49; sat up with Dr. Bayley during his illness, 49.

Protestant Sisters of Charity, 129.

Provoost, Rev. Bishop John, Episcopalian, New York City, witnessed marriage of Elizabeth Bayley and William M. Seton, 46.

Pyomingo, Setons return to New York on, 7, 76, 77; docked in New York, 8.

Sadler, Eliza, nick-named "Sad," early New York friend of Elizabeth Bayley Seton, 11; Bayley-Seton courtship in home of, 45; Elizabeth Seton's letter about Julia Scott to, 108; member of Widow's Society, 129; remained loyal to Elizabeth after her conversion to Catholicism, 130; Elizabeth longs for "Sad's" visit to St. Joseph's Valley, 130, 132, 134; loved by Elizabeth Seton's children, 133; Elizabeth's remembrances of, 134, 136; receives letter about Catherine Dupleix's visit to Elizabeth, 176; meeing with Father Cheverus, 137-138; grieved over Rebecca Seton's death, 138; Elizabeth's response to Sad, 139; Elizabeth relates views of faith to, 139; departure to Paris, 139; Elizabeth Seton's letter about Cecilia's and Harriet's death, 128.

Saint Aloysius Gonzaga, 13, 126.

Saint Andrew's Churchyard, burial place of Dr. Richard Bayley, 42.

Sain Joseph's Academy for Girls, title given to Elizabeth Seton's school in Emmitsburg, 13.

INDEX

Saint Joseph's Valley, permanent site of Elizabeth's school and religious community, 16, 165.
Saint Mark's Curate, 10.
Saint Mary's Chapel, dedication of, 12, 125; Sisters of Charity, wear habit for first time at Mass, 12.
Saint Mary's College, Baltimore, 14; attended by William and Richard Seton, 14; Rev. DuBourg president of, 125.
Saint Peter's Church, Barcla‧ Street, New York City; Rev. Matthew O'Brien at, 9; Rev. Michael Hur.. ; at, 12; Elizabeth Seton enters church, 85; Elizabeth Seton receives first Communion in, 86.
San Lorenzo, Florence, 72.
Santa Catarina, the church of, 8; Elizabeth Seton attends Mass before her departure from Leghorn, 8, 76.
Santa Maria Novella, Church of, Florence, 72.
Schools, William Harris', 10; Georgetown, 10; Montreal College, 10; Saint Mary's College, 10, 14; Mount Saint Mary's, 14.
Scott, Juliana (Julia), early friend of Dr. Richard Bayley and Elizabeth Seton, 6, 14, 34, 38, 101; writes Elizabeth Seton touching letter at Rebecca Seton's death (Elizabeth's sister-in-law), 100; receives letter from Elizabeth Seton in Emmitsburg, 19; lasting friendship with Elizabeth Seton, 101, 102; learns about Dr. Bayley's illness and death, 43; Elizabeth opens her heart freely to, 106, 110, 111, 112; befriends William M. Seton, 104, 140, sent box to Setons, 105; receives news about Elizabeth's children, 103; receives repeated invitations to visit Elizabeth on Long Island and in New York, 106, 107; invites Elizabeth Seton to Philadelphia, 107; Elizabeth declines invitation, 108; Elizabeth comforts Julia, 109, 110; Elizabeth tries to lift Julia's spirits, 111-113; remains faithful to Elizabeth, 115; boundless generosity shown to Sisters' orphanages in Philadelphia, 115; short visit to Emmitsburg, 116.
Seton, Anna Maria, eldest daughter of William Magee Seton and Elizabeth Bayley Seton, 4; accompanies parents to Italy, 5, 71; contracts scarlet fever, 74; in Baltimore, 133; illness of, 142; at New York City Battery, 94; love for Julia Scott, 105; receives money from Julia Scott, 115; romance of, 133; Bruté administers the Sacrament of Healing to, 142; death of, 142-143.
Seton, Catherine Josephine, fourth child of William and Elizabeth Seton, 4; left in care of sister-in-law Rebecca Seton, 5; at Saint Joseph's Academy, 14, 139; behavior during Dr. Bayley's illness, 41; image of Rebecca Seton, 94; receives money from Julia Scott, 116; enjoyed feeding lambs, 113; delights everybody, 105.
Seton, Cecilia, half-sister of William Magee Seton, 5, 11, 12, 13; Elizabeth Seton's inseparable friend, 117, 118, 122; Elizabeth counsels, 118; lives with Protestant relatives, 118; Elizabeth Seton longs for, 118; conversion to Catholicism, 119; persecuted by Protestant relatives, 119, 120; charged with James Seton's children, 120; encouraged by Elizabeth Seton,

120-124; learns importance of prayer and suffering, 124; fears separation from Elizabeth, 124; Elizabeth's account of journey to Baltimore for, 125; trek to Emmitsburg mountains, 127; moves to Stone House, 127; writes Father Babade, 127; conveyed to Baltimore, 127; death and burial of, 127-128.

Seton, Elizabeth Ann Bayley, background and early years, of, 8; learns to commune with God, 4; New York's "belle of the ball," 4; courtship with and marriage to William Magee Seton, 4, 45; confidante of father-in-law (William Seton, Esq.), 5, 91; mistress of Seton household, 4, 48; plans voyage to Leghorn, Italy, 5, 50-51; accompanies William to Italy, 5, 51; detained in Leghorn Lazaretto, 6, 52; keeps *Journal* for sister-in-law Rebecca Seton, 54; cares for William in Lazaretto, 56-60; transfer to Pisa, 64; at William's death bed, 65-68; guest of Antonio and Amabilia Filicchi, 69-76; learns about Catholic practices, 75; contracts scarlet fever from Anna, 75; received again into home of Antonio Filicchi, 75; departure delay deemed providential, 75; friendship bonds strengthened, 76, 80, 81; Elizabeth's desire to become a Catholic increases, 75; abandoned by Protestant friends, 79; meets Rev. DuBourg in New York, 10; accepts invitation to Emmitsburg, 10; illness of, 17, 18; death of, 18, 19; friendship with God, 21; learns to love nature, 22, 23; offers her children to God, 24; God reveals Himself in nature, 27; summer on Long Island, 24; longs for Rebecca Seton, 26; phenomena of nature give meaning to her life, 27-29; serves God faithfully, 29; makes covenant with God, 29; finds comfort in nature and friendships, 30, 31, 36; love for her father, 33-34, 38; addresses her father, *Mr. Monitor*, 36; lonesome during his absences, 37; defends her father, 37; uneasy about her father's health, 39; attends him during illness, 40; at her father's deathbed, 41; his spirit lives on in her, 44; heart-rending note to Dr. Moore, 42; letter to Julia Scott about Dr. Bayley, 43; writes Dr. Bayley's grave stone inscription, 43; spends happy hours with William Seton, 45, 46; concern over William's failing health, 47; concern over Seton-Maitland business failure, 48-50; quarantined in Leghorn Lazaretto, 53-63; prays and cares for William Seton, 58-63; kindness of Lazaretto capitano, 56, 60, 61; reads Bible to William, 58, 60, 63; sends for Dr. Tutilli, 60; resigned to God's will, 62, 65; writes Rebecca about William's suffering, 64; inspires William to love God, 63-66; gratitude on leaving Lazaretto, 64; at William's last agony, 67; thanks God for William's release, 68; prepares William's body for burial, 68; interment in Leghorn, 68; aftermath of William's death, 69; stays with Filicchis, 69; visits William's grave, 70; tours Florence, 71-72; receives letter from Antonio, 73; begins close friendship with Antonio Filicchi, 73; return voyage on *Shepherdess* delayed, 74; visits shrines in Montenero, 75; learns more about the Catholic faith, 76; return passage on *Pyomingo*, 76; bids farewell to Filicchis, 76; accompanied by Antonio Filicchi, 77; temptations on board ship, 78; arrival in New York, 79;

INDEX

desires to become a Catholic, 79; looks to Antonio for encouragment, 79; writes Antonio Filicchi in Boston, 79; receives letter from Antonio, 80; struggles with the faith, 82-84; disturbed by Newton's *Prophecies*, 82; devotion to the Blessed Virgin Mary, 82; rereads Saint Francis de Sales and the *Lives of the Saints* and others, 84; awakened by Bourdaloue's homily on Epiphany, 85; writes Rev. John Cheverus for advice, 85; enters the Church, 86; receives First Communion, 86; gratitude to Antonio Filicchi, 86; support of friends after conversion, 87; letters and good wishes to Antonio, 88; prays for a never-ending friendship in heaven, 88; writes Julia Scott about Rebecca Seton, her sister-in-law, 91; fascinated by Rebecca Seton, 92; desired Rebecca's company, 92; writes about her children to Rebecca, 94; sends a message to Rebecca concerning Rev. Mr. Hobart, 94; tells Rebecca about William's poor health, 95; concern for Rebecca, 96; describes yellow fever suffering, 97; shares good news with Rebecca, 98; writes Rebecca from New York Harbor, 98; keeps *Journal* for Rebecca, 99; writes about William's death, 100; finds Rebecca ill, 100; at death bed of Rebecca Seton, 100; Julia Scott, an early friend of, 101; speaks of Julia Scott about religion, 102; writes Julia Scott about William Seton, 104, 105; expects visit from Julia Scott, 106; grief at Doctor Bayley's death, 106; invites Julia to visit her, 106; shares Julia's sorrows, 108; anxious about Julia's dejected spirits, 109; advises Julia, 109; shares her sorrows with Julia, 110, 113; writes Julia about heaven and death, 114; writes Julia about Mammy Huler's death, 114; keeps Julia always in her heart, 115; special fondness for Cecilia Seton, 117; teaches Cecilia her prayers, 117; concern for Cecilia, 118; wishes to see Cecilia, 118; supports Cecilia after conversion to Catholicism, 119; relates her experiences to Cecilia Seton, 120-121; shares Cecilia's sufferings, "a prisoner of the Lord," 122; counsels Cecilia Seton, 122-124; writes Cecilia account of journey to Baltimore, 125; prepares for Cecilia Seton's arrival, 126; journey to Emmitsburg, 127; writes Father DuBourg, 127; sojourn at Mount Saint Mary's, 127; death of Cecilia and Harriet Seton, 128; establishes St. Joseph's Academy, 129; founds religious community, 129; friendship with Catherine Dupleix (Dué) and Eliza Sadler (Sad), 129; invites Dué and Sad to Emmitsburg, 130, 132, 133, 134; writes about her children to Dué and Sad, 131, 132, 133; disappointed by Sad, 135; learns about Dué's conversion, 135; joy at Dué's visit to Saint Joseph's, 136; concern over Sad's eternal happiness, 136-138; receives Sad's letter, 138; affirms her love for Sad, 139; remembers Dué and Sad at Mass, 140; meets Rev. Simon G. Bruté in Emmitsburg, 141; writes about Bruté to Archbishop Carroll, 142; finds kindred spirit in Bruté, 142; helps Bruté with English, 143; loves the priesthood, 145; opens her heart freely to Bruté, 146; writes about Bruté to Antonio Filicchi, 147, 148; advises Bruté, 148; prays for Bruté, 151, 152; friendship with Bruté, 150, 152, 156-157; failing health of, 157, 158; receives Sacrament of Healing, 157; death and burial of, 158.

Seton, Harriet, half-sister of William Magee Seton, 5, 11, 12; accompanies Cecilia to Baltimore, 126; moves to Emmitsburg, 126; converted to Catholicism, 13, 188:22; illness and death of, 183:9; burial of, 183:9; Annina decks the grave of, 133.

Seton, James, brother of William Magee Seton, 98; husband of Mary Hoffman Seton, 16; house on Greenwich Street, 98; invites Cecilia Seton to care for his children, 120, 121, 124.

Seton-Maitland & Company, in care of William Magee Seton, 4; foreclosures in London and Hamburg by Maitland, 4, 48, 49; bankruptcy filed, 5, 129; settlement of business affairs, 98.

Seton, Mary Hoffman, wife of James Seton, painful death-bed scene of, 16; Elizabeth Seton at death bed of, 16.

Seton, Rebecca, youngest child of Elizabeth and William Magee Seton, 4; in care of Elizabeth Seton's sister, Mary Post, 5; in Emmitsburg, 14; lameness of, 16, 153; death of, 16; cherished by Catherine Dupleix (Dué), 131; favors Dué, 131; Fr. Bruté's affection for, 153; loves Bruté, 154; Bruté at bedside of, 154; Elizabeth's letter to Bruté about Rebecca's death, 155.

Seton, Rebecca, half-sister of William Magee Seton, 5; friendship with Elizabeth Seton, 92, 93, 95; member of Ladies of Charity society, 93; inspired by Rev. Mr. Hobart, 94; poor health of, 96; cares for Elizabeth Seton's children, 51; at brother Jack's house, 92, 96; Leghorn *Journal* written for, 54, 98, 99; Elizabeth's description of yellow fever scenes for, 97; at Mary Seton's deathbed, 97; cared for Eliza Maitland and family, 97; last illness of, 100; Elizabeth Seton at death bed of, 100; receives note from Elizabeth leaving the New York Harbor, 51.

Seton, Richard, second son of Elizabeth and William Magee Seton, 4; in the care of Elizabeth's sister-in-law, Rebecca Seton, 5; at Georgetown College, 10; transferred to Mount St. Mary's College, 14; named for Dr. Richard Bayley, 36; at New York City Battery, 94; illness of, 112; Dr. Bayley saves life of, 112; Julia Scott's kindness to, 116; love for Catherine Dupleix, 131; asks questions about Elizabeth Seton's friends and New York connections, 133; obtains position in Baltimore assisted by Bruté, 152-153.

Seton, Samuel, half-brother of William M. Seton, accompanies Cecilia and Harriet to Baltimore, 126.

Seton, William, Esq., international merchant, 4; father-in-law of Elizabeth Bayley Seton, 4; founder and director of Seton-Maitland shipping firm, 4, 48; favors Elizabeth Seton as confidante, 5, 48, 91; mishap and death of, 48; leaves large family in care of Elizabeth Seton, 91.

Seton, William, second child and son of Elizabeth Seton, in care of Elizabeth's sister-in-law, Rebecca Seton, 5; at Georgetown College, 10; at Mount St. Mary's College, 14; at New York City Battery, 94; accompanied to Europe by Rev. Simon G. Bruté on *Tontine*, 147, helped by Mr. Preudhomme de Borre in Marseilles, 148; writes to Bruté in France, 148; love for Dué (Catherine Dupleix), 131; enjoys Julia (Aunt) Scott, 105; receives gifts

INDEX

from Julia Scott, 116; received kindly by the Filicchis, 149; receives letter in Leghorn from Bruté about Rebecca's death, 154.

Seton, William Magee, ancestry of, 4; courtship and marriage with Elizabeth Bayley, 4, 45; love of music, 46; joy with Elizabeth and children, 46, 47; failing health of, 47, 50, 52; family representative of Seton mercantile interests, 48; business failure of Seton-Maitland firm, 49; voyage to Leghorn, Italy with Elizabeth, 51; set sail on *Shepherdess*, 51; Seton's arrival in Leghorn, 52; detained at Leghorn Lazaretto, 53, 61; kindness of Filicchis, 53, 56; prays with Elizabeth in Lazaretto, 58, 62, 67; suffers severe attacks, 60; visited by friends, 59, 60, 61; conversion of, 62; removal to Pisa, 64; health worsens, 65-66; last illness and death of, 67, 68; burial in English Protestant cemetery, Leghorn, 69; sympathy of friends, 69.

Shepherdess, Setons embark for Leghorn, Italy, 5; return voyage delayed, 7, 75.

Sisters of Charity of Saint Joseph's, religious community founded by Elizabeth Seton, Baltimore, Maryland, 12; wear habit for the first time, 12; transfer to Emmitsburg, Maryland, 13, 127; greeted by Rev. John DuBois at Mount Saint Mary's, 13, 127; moved to the Stone House, 13, 127; White House, 13; community grows, 14; Fr. DuBourg, first superior, 125, 127; Carroll's preference, 15; DuBois adapts French rules for, 141; Bruté's interest in, 142; gratitude to Bruté, 191:39.

Stone House, farmhouse on Fleming Farm, 13.

Sulpician Retreat House, first shelter of Elizabeth Seton and Sisters in Emmitsburg, 13.

Tessier, Rev. John, S.S., superior at Saint Mary's Seminary, appoints Fr. Bruté to Mount Saint Mary's College, Emmitsburg, 150.

Tillary, Dr. James, attended Dr. Richard Bayley at death, 41.

Tisserant, Rev. John S., New York friend of Elizabeth Seton, suggests William and Richard attend Georgetown College, 11.

Tontine, sails for Bordeaux, 147; William Seton aboard accompanied by Bruté, 147.

Trinity Church, New York City, 62, 75, 99.

Tutilli, Doctor, friend of Antonio Filicchi, visits William Magee Seton in Lazaretto, 56, 65; diagnoses Anna Maria's illness on board ship, 75.

Weis, George, Baltimore friend and confidant of Elizabeth Seton, 17; Elizabeth's affection for, 179; Elizabeth sends messages of love to his wife, Minon, 179; serves Elizabeth Seton's needs, 179.

White House, the permanent home of Elizabeth Seton's school and community, 13.

White, Patrick, educator from Albany, New York, attempts to establish school in Elizabeth Seton's New York home, 10.

White, Sister Rose, Sister of Charity, nominated to replace Elizabeth Ann Seton as mother of the community, 17.

Widow's Society, organized for the relief of the poor, 129.
Yellow fever epidemic, 36, 39, 48, 54, 68; Elizabeth's account of epidemic to Julia Scott, 39; Dr. Richard Bayley's interest in, 36, 37; Dr. Richard Bayley dies of, 41; fear of, 48, 68; victims' sufferings from, 97.